HISTORIC KIRTLAND

GUIDE FOR TRAVEL AND STUDY

Explore more Church History Sites in
the Search, Ponder, Pray Series:

New England Guide for Travel and Study

Missouri Guide for Travel and Study

Illinois Guide for Travel and Study

DAMON BAHR & THOMAS AARDEMA

HISTORIC KIRTLAND

GUIDE FOR TRAVEL AND STUDY

This is not an official publication of The Church of Jesus Christ of Latter-day Saints. The opinions and views expressed herein belong solely to the author and do not necessarily represent the opinions or views of Cedar Fort, Inc. Permission for the use of sources, graphics, and photos is also solely the responsibility of the author.

ISBN 13: 978-1-4621-4389-4

Published by CFI, an imprint of Cedar Fort, Inc.
2373 W. 700 S., Suite 100, Springville, UT 84663
Distributed by Cedar Fort, Inc., www.cedarfort.com

Cover design by Courtney Proby
Cover design © 2023 Cedar Fort, Inc.
Edited by Casey Paul Griffiths & Mary Jane Woodger

Printed in Colombia

10 9 8 7 6 5 4 3 2 1

Printed on acid-free paper

Kirtland has become my home and I couldn't be more grateful for so many experiences that have left an indelible impression upon me and helped me recognize more fully that this is sacred soil. These sites are part of the Lord's restoration of his Church. Kirtland played such an important role in the rolling forth of the Kingdom of God. I hope that each visitor will come to love Kirtland and strengthen their witness and understanding of the restored Gospel of Jesus Christ. I am grateful for my wife Emilee and our five boys for their willingness to make Ohio our home. I am grateful for Damon Bahr and his knowledge, faith, and talent and for his passion for all things Kirtland. Its inspiring to write with him. I am grateful for everyone who has helped me fall in love with church history and instilled in me a passion to share Kirtland with everyone. This book is dedicated to them. Thank you.

—Thomas P. Aardema

The production of a book always involves so many people, all of whom deserve thanks. I am grateful to my wife, Kim, and our children, for always supporting me in projects such as this book. I also appreciate Tommy Aardema, my co-author, who has a great sense for the type of writing this book entails. I am grateful to Casey Griffiths for his leadership in this project, and for his support of our book, and to the fine folks at Cedar Fort who have been so great to work with. We have so many friends in the Kirtland area who have touched our lives, so any book such as this clearly has their imprint.

—Damon L. Bahr

CONTENTS

Introduction

The First Gathering Place

If New England is the cradle of the restoration, Ohio is the place where the infant Church took its first steps and learned its most important childhood lessons. Just as a child rapidly grows and experiences its first words, first steps, and other milestones, the number of firsts experienced by the Church in Ohio illustrates what an important time of development the Ohio period was for the Church. The first bishop was called in February 1831. The First Presidency was organized in January 1832. The Quorums of the Twelve and the Seventy were organized in February 1835. Perhaps crowning all of these achievements was the first temple being dedicated in Kirtland, Ohio in March 1836, and was visited personally by the firstborn Son of God along with a host of other angelic ministers.

The appearance of Jesus Christ in the Kirtland Temple was just one of several places where not only the Savior, but where the Father and the Son, appeared together to the early Saints. Diverse locations including the farms of Isaac Morley and John Johnson became sacred sites by the appearances of the Father and the Son. The most notable testimonies of these appearances to Joseph Smith and his close associates in the work were recorded in Ohio. On February 16, 1832, Joseph and Sidney Rigdon saw Jesus Christ and God side by side, writing, "And now, after the many testimonies which have been given of him, this is the testimony, last of all, which we give of him: That he lives!" (Doctrine and Covenants 76:22).

The amount of revelation received in Kirtland is staggering. Dozens of revelations, forming over half of the Doctrine and Covenants were received in Kirtland. Here Joseph Smith and his scribes completed their new translation of the Bible. These revelations illuminated concepts like consecration, the importance of education, the basics of Church government and the majesty of Jesus Christ and His redeeming mission. The work of the Church around the world today still rest on the foundation of the revelation received in Ohio. The Ohio period began with a commandment to the Saints to gather there in promise of a law and an endowment of power (Doctrine and Covenants 38:32). The endowment poured out in Ohio still blesses the lives of millions around the world today. A few days visiting the sacred sites of Ohio demonstrates to the observer the suffering of the early Saints, but also the blessings poured out upon them. Every promise of the gathering was fulfilled. Even as the Saints were forced to flee Ohio they acknowledged the rich blessings that had been poured out in this place.

Why We Wrote This Book

This book is part of a series of guides designed to enhance your visit to Church History sites. This book focuses on Church history sites in Ohio, where the Prophet Joseph Smith and his family lived from 1831 to 1838. In Ohio Joseph Smith received many of his most important revelations and developed some of his most important friendships. Visiting the homes where the

Prophet and these heroic early Saints lived is a wonderful way to make their stories come alive. Two wonderful historians, Thomas P. Aardema and Damon L. Bahr wrote the material used in this book. Both of them have years of experience with the sacred sites in Ohio, and we are deeply grateful for their contributions. They have written in even greater depth about the revelations received in Ohio in their book *The Voice of the Lord is Unto All Men: A Remarkable Year of Revelations in the John Johnson Home.*[1] They are among the finest guides available to the Ohio sites of the Restoration.

However, any site become just another stop on the road without a knowledge of the history that took place there. Many of the sites have visitor centers staffed by helpful missionaries who can assist you in knowing the story that makes the place sacred. Many pilgrims enlist the help of a guide during the travels through the lands of the Restoration. On occasion, during our visits to the sites we have often seen families pull up to site, wander a few moments, and then return to car without fully knowing what makes the place they visited so special.

In the past many site books were concerned with just helping you find the site. With the advent of new technology, finding most of the Church history sites is relatively simple. This has rapidly increased the number of people who seek out the sites on their own. Because of this, directions to the sites have been placed in this book only when they are absolutely necessary. Instead, these books are designed to provide you with the stories behind the sites. Whenever possible we have drawn from first-hand sources produced by the people who lived on these properties and played their vital roles in the work of the Restoration. The intent behind these books is to enhance your visits to the sites by putting primary sources into your grasp, arranged site by site.

Another notable departure in these books is the scope we have chosen. Many guidebooks have chosen to list every site possible within a given area. This can be very useful, but this usually limits the book to just a few paragraphs because of the need to cover every site. Where other books have chosen breadth over depth, we have chosen instead to focus on the primary sites in each region and provide a thorough account of the events there from primary sources. That means that there might be many places worth visiting not in the book. Not far from Kirtland, for example, is a site where the first baptisms took place. This site is difficult to find but well worth visiting and you might want to consult with the local missionaries if you are interested in more out of

---

1	Damon L. Bahr and Thomas P. Aardema, *The Voice of the Lord is Unto All Men: A Remarkable Year of Revelations in the John Johnson Home,* (Springville, UT: Cedar Fort Publishing and Media, 2021).

the way sites like this one. For our purposes here, we have chosen to focus on the primary sites in each region.

How to Use This Book

This book is arranged to give you the stories that took place at each of the sites, with special emphasis on the relationship of each location to the scriptures, particularly the Doctrine and Covenants. Chapters are arranged roughly chronologically, beginning with Kirtland, the first place Joseph Smith lived during his time in Ohio, and continuing with other places the Prophet made his own, including the first home he and his wife Emma Hale Smith built together. Other books in the series will cover the Church history sites and their stories in New England, Missouri, Illinois, and other locations.

Each chapter begins with a few bullet points which overview the most significant events at each site, and the revelations received at these locations. The story behind the site is organized around these events, with emphasis given to the times and places where revelations were received that became part of the scriptural canon. Many of the Ohio sites, such as the Kirtland Historic Site and the John Johnson Farm, are staffed by missionaries who can help guide you through the sites. These books are not intended to take the place of the missionaries, whose testimonies and teaching you will find to be an important part of each site visit. The missionaries at the sites will help you find the key locations and share brief stories with you. These books are designed to enhance the experience you will have with the missionaries by providing you with the primary sources and cutting edge scholarship for each of the locations.

Other sites, such as the Isaac Morley Farm or Fairport Harbor do not have missionaries and can be more difficult to find. Information at these sites can be challenging to find, so we have included photographs and more specific directions to find these sites. At these locations the information in this book will help you act as your own tour guide, or a guide to others. Sites without visitor centers or missionaries are often overlooked but can provide an array of edifying experiences if visitors are provided with the right information.

Casey Paul Griffiths
Mary Jane Woodger
General Editors

Significant events at this location:

- In 1798, Moses Cleveland, on behalf of the Connecticut Land Company, surveyed the Kirtland area with the intention of forming a township.

- In 1799, Turhand Kirtland was given a portion of acreage that became Kirtland Township.

- In 1826, Sidney Rigdon became the pastor of the Reformed Baptist congregation in Mentor, Ohio.

- In November 1830, the first missionaries of the Church in the Kirtland area converted over a hundred local settlers, including Sidney Rigdon.

- In December 1830, Lord commanded Joseph Smith and Sidney Rigdon to "go to the Ohio" (see Doctrine and Covenants 37).

- In February 1831, Joseph and Emma Smith moved to Kirtland. During their time in Ohio, they lived with the families of Newel K. and Elizabeth Ann Whitney, Isaac and Lucy Morley, and John and Elsa Johnson.

- In the winter of 1833–34, Joseph and Emma Smith moved to their own home near the site of the Kirtland Temple, which was then under construction.

- On March 27, 1836, the Kirtland Temple was dedicated.

- On April 3, 1836, Jesus Christ and the ancient prophets Moses, Elias, and Elijah appeared to Joseph Smith and Oliver Cowdery in the Kirtland Temple.

- In January 1838, Joseph Smith and his family fled Kirtland following a serious apostasy of Church members who were involved in a financial crisis. After this time, Kirtland ceased to function as a meaningful center for the Church.

"The Ohio": Successful Missionary Work in the Kirtland Area

The visitor's center at Historic Kirtland.
Photo by Acacia E. Griffiths.

The Land of Kirtland

In September 1830, the Lord issued a general call for the elect to "be gathered in unto one place" (Doctrine and Covenants 29:8). Three months later in December 1830, the Lord revealed a specific place: "They should assemble together at the Ohio" (Doctrine and Covenants 37:3). This revelation was the "first commandment concerning a gathering in this dispensation" (Doctrine and Covenants 37, section heading). At that time, the two hundred or more members of the Church located in the Palmyra, Fayette, and Colesville branches in New York were experiencing intense opposition, while new converts were flocking to the gospel in Kirtland, Ohio, and the surrounding area.

The Stoney Brook near the Historic Kirtland Visitor Center.

The Lord had begun preparing northeast Ohio as a gathering place for his Saints many years before Joseph Smith and Sidney Rigdon received Doctrine and Covenants 37. Northeast Ohio is located on the northern edge of the Allegheny Plateau, which was included in the four million acres of land that King Charles II of England dedicated to the Connecticut Colony in 1630. Following the American Revolution, the State of Connecticut exchanged some acreage on this land for federal assumption of its debt accrued during the war, and the remaining 3,366,921 acres on the northwest corner became known as the Western Reserve. The westernmost 500,000 acres was known as the Firelands, which the State of Connecticut set aside to compensate its citizens whose property had been destroyed by the British during the war. In 1796 the remaining 1.2 million acres on the eastern side were sold to a group of private speculators known as the Connecticut Land Company.[2]

2   "Connecticut Land Company," Ohio History Central, Ohio History
      Connection, accessed August 10, 2022, http://www.ohiohistorycentral.org/w/
      Connecticut_Land_Company.

By 1798, expeditions sponsored by the Connecticut Land Company and led by Moses Cleveland began surveying this densely forested frontier. Turhand Kirtland, one of the surveyors, received a portion of the land, later named Kirtland Township, as payment for his work. By the fall of 1799, Turhand began selling parcels of land to settlers in the area. Among these early settlers were Isaac and Lucy Morley and Newel K. and Elizabeth Ann Whitney, who would later join the Church and contribute significantly to its early history. While Kirtland's economy was based primarily on agriculture, there were also a number of waterwheel-powered mills and factories on the east branch of the Chagrin River, an area the locals referred to as "Kirtland Mills."[3]

Conversions of Sidney Rigdon and Parley P. Pratt

Sidney Rigdon preached at this chapel in Mantua, Ohio, one of the oldest Disciples Churches in the region. Photo by Acacia E. Griffiths.

---

3   "Kirtland Mills" (geographical entry), JSP.

The entrance to the Mantua Center Christian Church, a congregation Sidney Rigdon was affiliated with before his conversion. Photo by Acacia E. Griffiths.

This pulpit in the Mantua Christian Center was in use in the 1820s and may have been used by Sidney Rigdon in his preaching. Photo by Casey Paul Griffiths

In the early 1800s, "an unusual excitement on the subject of religion" (Joseph Smith—History 1:5) swept through northern Ohio, along with western New York and northern Pennsylvania, led by Methodists, Presbyterians, and Baptists. Among those stirring up this "unusual excitement" was Sidney Rigdon,[4] a Baptist convert who associated himself with the Restorationist movement led by Walter Scott and Alexander Campbell, whose followers were known as Reform Baptists or Campbellites. He eventually qualified himself to become a licensed preacher with the Regular Baptists and began preaching in 1819 in Trumbull County, Ohio. There he married Phebe Brooks and then moved to Pennsylvania in 1821 where he was appointed pastor of the First Baptist Church in Pittsburgh and became well known for his dynamic preaching. However, because Sidney did not agree with the Baptist doctrine of infant damnation, he ceased preaching for the Baptists in 1824. He then worked as a tanner in Pennsylvania until 1826 when he moved his family to Ohio. Sidney began preaching as a Restorationist preacher in Mentor, Ohio, that same year, although he was no longer authorized by the Regular Baptists. In 1830, Sidney broke with the Reform Baptists and Campbellites because of differences over having "all things in common" (Acts 4:32) and receiving spiritual gifts, and he began to lead congregations designated as "Rigdonites." One of Sidney's proselytes was Parley P. Pratt.

While preaching of a future gospel restoration, Sidney Rigdon was unaware that the Lord had already begun restoring his Church to the earth in western New York and northern Pennsylvania. Nor was he aware that the Lord was directing him as an instrument to help prepare the way for the restored gospel to come to "the Ohio." Through divine orchestration, Sidney's and Parley's friendship would be key in fulfilling that preparatory work.

In the summer of 1830, Parley P. Pratt felt impressed to sell his home in Amherst, Ohio, and travel to New York to preach the gospel. Having only $10, Parley and his wife, Thankful, traveled by boat from Cleveland, Ohio, to Buffalo, New York, and on the Erie Canal toward Albany, New York.[5] Along the way, Parley felt prompted to leave the canal boat at Newark, New York, ten miles east of Palmyra, leaving Thankful to travel alone toward their final destination.

---

4   "History of Joseph Smith," *The Times and Seasons* 4, no. 12 (May 1, 1843): 177, https://contentdm.lib.byu.edu/digital/collection/NCMP1820-1846/id/8500.

5   *The Autobiography of Parley Parker Pratt, One of the Twelve Apostles of the Church of Jesus Christ of Latter-day Saints: Embracing His Life, Ministry and Travels, With Extracts, in Prose and Verse, From His Miscellaneous Writings*, ed. Parley P. Pratt (Chicago: Law, King & Law, 1888), 36.

I informed my wife that, notwithstanding our passage being paid through the whole distance, yet I must leave the boat and her to pursue her passage to our friends; while I would stop awhile in the region. Why, I did not know; but so it was plainly manifest by the Spirt to me. I said to her, "we part for a season; go and visit our friends in our native place; I will come soon, but how soon I know not; for I have a work to do in this region of country, and what it is, or how long it will take to perform it, I know not; but I will come when it is performed."[6]

After just a few days, Parley was introduced to the Book of Mormon by a Baptist deacon named Hamblin, which dramatically changed the course of his life. He later wrote, "I read all day; eating was a burden, I had no desire for food; sleep was a burden when the night came, for I preferred reading to sleep. . . . I knew and comprehended that the book was true. . . . My joy was now full."[7]

Parley then traveled to Palmyra hoping to meet the Joseph Smith, but he instead found the Prophet's brother Hyrum who taught him the gospel. He was baptized by Oliver Cowdery on September 1, 1830. Ultimately Parley's conversion led to the conversion of Sidney Rigdon and also led to the subsequent gathering of the New York and Pennsylvania Saints to Kirtland.

---

6   *Autobiography of Parley Parker Pratt*, 36–37.
7   *Autobiography of Parley Parker Pratt*, 38.

Missionary Success in Kirtland

Historic records indicate that this spot in the Chagrin River is where the first baptisms in the Kirtland area took place. Photo by Acacia E. Griffiths.

During the month of Parley's baptism, a conflict arose regarding revelation and Church governance. Hiram Page, an in-law of the Whitmer family, claimed to be receiving revelation for the Church through a seer stone. Despite the fact that on the day the Church was organized the Lord had directed the Saints to "give heed unto all [Joseph's] words and commandments which he shall give unto [them] as he receiveth them" (Doctrine and Covenants 21:4), Hiram influenced many Church members, including Oliver Cowdery.

The Page deception was no small matter for Joseph Smith. As he sought divine help just before a Church conference in September 1830, the Lord spoke through Joseph to Oliver Cowdery: "No one shall be appointed to receive commandments and revelations in this church excepting my servant Joseph Smith, Jun." (Doctrine and Covenants 28:2). The Lord then directed Oliver to tell Hiram Page "that those things which he hath written from that stone are not of [God]" (verses 11–12, 14). Perhaps expressing faith in Oliver despite his error, the Lord called Oliver on a mission to "go unto the Lamanites" (verse 8), to "the borders by the Lamanites" (verse 9), the area where the western border of the new state of Missouri met the unincorporated Indian Territory that later became the state of Kansas. In this same revelation, the Lord also revealed the general location of the city of Zion.

Three other brethren were called to serve as Oliver Cowdery's companions (see Doctrine and Covenants 30, 32). The first to be called was Peter Whitmer Jr., a son of Peter Sr. and Mary Whitmer, the couple whose home was a refuge for the Prophet and Oliver while they completed the Book of Mormon translation. The Whitmer home was also the place where the Church was formally organized. Oliver and Peter were joined by Parley P. Pratt and Ziba Peterson, a convert who served two missions with Oliver but remained active in the Church for only two or three years. Feeling bolstered by the Lord's promise "I myself will go with them" (Doctrine and Covenants 32:3), the four missionary companions carried carpet bags full of copies of the Book of Mormon. They left New York in early October 1830 and traveled about 1,500 miles, mostly on foot, to Missouri, preaching to various Native American tribes along the way. Their arrival in Missouri was an important event in Church history, but their stop in Ohio on the way became a pivotal moment that would change the course of Church development.

While traveling through northern Ohio, Parley P. Pratt suggested they visit his former religious mentor, Sidney Rigdon. Initially the missionaries had very little success in the Kirtland area, including limited response from Sidney and his congregation. However, Parley reported the following: "The people thronged us night and day, insomuch that we had no time for rest and retirement. . . . Thousands flocked about us daily; some to be taught, some for curiosity, some to obey the gospel, and some to dispute or resist it."[8] According to Parley, during the three weeks the missionaries were in the area, 127 people were baptized,[9] including Sidney and about one hundred members of his congregation in Mentor.

Sidney Rigdon's conversion meant sacrificing a popular, influential, and lucrative position for a second time. "At present, the honors and applause of the world were showered down upon him, his wants were abundantly supplied, and anticipated. . . . But if he should unite with the Church of Christ, his prospects of wealth and affluence would vanish; his family dependent upon him for support, must necessarily share his humiliation and poverty."[10] Sidney and his wife, Phoebe, weighed carefully the risk and the reason. "'My Dear, you have once followed me into poverty, are you again willing to do the same?' She then

---

8   *Autobiography of Parley Parker Pratt*, 50.

9   *Autobiography of Parley Parker Pratt*, 50.

10   "History of Joseph Smith," *The Latter-day Saints' Millenial Star* 5, no. 2 (July 1844): 17, https://contentdm.lib.byu.edu/digital/collection/MStar/id/293.

said—'I have weighed the matter, I have contemplated the circumstances in which we may be placed; I have counted the cost, and I am perfectly satisfied to follow you; it is my desire to do the will of God, come life or come death.'"[11]

The four missionaries then continued their journey west, leaving the new converts to the leadership of their fellow converts who had been called to preside over branches in the area: Isaac Morley (later replaced by John Whitmer) in Kirtland, Sidney Rigdon in Mentor, John Murdock in Warrensville, and an unknown leader in perhaps a fourth branch in Mayfield.[12] Missionary work also continued as the new converts preached the gospel in northern Ohio, some without formal mission calls. By February 2, 1831, a total of about four hundred people had joined the Church, and approximately seventy of them had been baptized by John Murdock.[13]

Desiring to meet Joseph Smith in person, Sidney Rigdon and an interested investigator and friend, Edward Partridge of nearby Painesville, traveled to New York in December 1830. After meeting the Prophet, Edward was baptized, and Joseph subsequently received two revelations, one for each new convert. Addressing Sidney, the Lord compared him to John the Baptist and honored the work he had done before his conversion. "Behold thou wast sent forth, even as John, to prepare the way before me, and before Elijah which should come, and thou knewest it not" (Doctrine and Covenants 35:11). Sidney was unaware of his fundamental role in the Restoration. Establishing his congregation in northeast Ohio had prepared the area for the gathering of the Saints to Ohio, where the Lord continued to restore the fullness of the gospel. Sidney had taught his congregation "restoration doctrine," which prepared his followers to listen to the four missionaries when they stopped briefly in Ohio.

In December 1830, Joseph Smith struggled to deal with the constant and vicious persecution he and the Saints were facing in New York and northern Pennsylvania. After hearing that the gospel was rapidly gaining strength in Ohio, he petitioned the Lord in prayer and received the revelation now found in Doctrine and Covenants 37 that the Saints "should assemble together at the Ohio." On January 2, 1831, the Prophet read this revelation to the members

---

11   History of Joseph Smith, *The Latter-day Saints' Millenial Star*, 5 no. 2 (July 1844): 17, https://contentdm.lib.byu.edu/digital/collection/MStar/id/293.

12   "Mayfield Township, Ohio" (geographical entry), The Joseph Smith Papers, accessed August 27, 2022, https://www.josephsmithpapers.org/place/mayfield-township-ohio.

13   John Murdock, journal, 1792–1864, Harold B. Lee Library, Brigham Young University, accessed December 17, 2019, http://boap.org/LDS/Early-Saints/JMurdock.html.

who were participating in a conference of the Church in Fayette. Joseph then received two additional revelations wherein the Lord reiterated his command to "go to the Ohio" (Doctrine and Covenants 38:32). The Lord also promised, "Inasmuch as my people shall assemble themselves at the Ohio, I have kept in store a blessing such as is not known among the children of men" (Doctrine and Covenants 39:15).

Gathering

The lighthouse at Fairport Harbor, Ohio. Many of the Saints gathering from New England first arrived in Ohio at this harbor. Photo by Casey Paul Griffiths.

To assess the condition of the Ohio Saints, the Prophet directed John Whitmer to be the first to move Kirtland and instructed him to do what he could to strengthen them. John arrived in Kirtland mid-January 1831. Joseph and Emma Smith left for Kirtland by sleigh on January 24. Emma was pregnant with twins, so a young woman, whose name is unknown, traveled with the Smiths to assist Emma along the way. Sidney Rigdon, Edward Partridge, Ezra Thayre, and Joseph Knight Sr. also accompanied the Smiths, traveling in a wagon full of copies of the Book of Mormon. Since the wagon moved slowly,

Sidney went on ahead of the group and arrived in Kirtland on January 30. The rest of the company arrived sometime between February 1 and 4.[14]

Most of the remaining New York and Pennsylvania Saints followed the Lord's command to gather to Ohio. However, as Newel Knight wrote, they "were obliged to make great sacrifices of [their] property."[15] They traveled with members of one of the three local branches: the Palmyra branch led by Martin Harris,[16] the Fayette branch by Thomas B. Marsh[17] and Lucy Mack Smith,[18] and the Colesville branch by Newel Knight.[19] These 200 Saints joined the 400 Ohio converts, and by the time the Missouri migrations began in June 1831, well over 1,000 members were living in Ohio.[20]

As the population of Saints in Kirtland continued to increase during the first three months following the Prophet's arrival, the Lord revealed that he would "retain a strong hold in the land of Kirtland, for the space of five years" (Doctrine and Covenants 64:21). In that five-year period, Joseph Smith received nearly half of the revelations found in the Doctrine and Covenants and completed most of the inspired translation of the Bible. Most of the priesthood offices and quorums were formalized and filled; missionaries were sent into the eastern United States, Canada, and England, bringing thousands into the kingdom; and a temple was built wherein priesthood keys were restored and the initiatory portion of the endowment was administered. Evidence suggests there may have been as many as sixty-one Church branches in the area surrounding Kirtland by the time the Saints left.[21]

During the Kirtland period, Joseph and Emma Smith lived in many places. They first stayed in the home of Newel K. and Elizabeth Ann Whitney in Kirtland, then they moved to a house on the Isaac and Lucy Morley farm in Mentor, and then they resided in the home of John and Elsa Johnson in Hiram. After that first year, the Smiths moved back to Kirtland to live in the

14   Mark Lyman Staker, *Hearken O Ye People: The Historical Setting of Joseph Smith's Ohio Revelations* (Salt Lake City: Greg Kofford Books, 2009), 96.

15   Newel Knight, autobiography and journal, circa 1846, MS 767, Church History Library, Salt Lake City.

16   "Martin Harris" (biographical entry), The Joseph Smith Papers, accessed August 27, 2022, .https://www.josephsmithpapers.org/person/martin-harris

17   "Thomas Baldwin Marsh" (biographical entry), JSP.

18   "Lucy Mack Smith" (biographical entry), JSP.

19   "Newel Knight" (biographical entry), JSP.

20   *Autobiography of Parley Parker Pratt*, 64.

21   Karl Ricks Anderson, "The Western Reserve," in *Mapping Mormonism*, ed. Brandon S. Plewe, S. Kent Brown, Donald Q. Cannon, and Richard H. Jackson (Provo, UT: BYU Press, 2012), 28–29.

Whitney store before eventually moving into their own home just north of the Kirtland Temple site in 1833.

Mini-Devotional – "Gather to the Ohio"

The command given to gather to Ohio (Doctrine and Covenants 37:1-3) is the first time the Saints were commanded to gather together. During the 19th century the doctrine of gathering was one of the most unique features of the religion of the Latter-day Saints. Coverts gathered from locations around the globe to places like Ohio, Missouri, Illinois, and the Western North America in obedience the Lord's command to gather. Building centers of strength allowed the early Saints to accomplish goals they would have not been able to achieve without on their own. As part of the gathering the first temple was built in Kirtland Ohio. Later Church leaders instructed the Saints to gather to their own lands, opening the door to the construction of hundreds of temple around the globe. Take a moment to discuss or reflect on the following:

- Does the doctrine of gathering still apply in our day?
- What are some ways that the Saints still heed the Lord's command to gather?
- Why is it important for the Saints gather together?

Significant events at this location:

- On September 12, 1832, Joseph and Emma Smith, and their first child, Julia Murdock Smith, moved from Hiram, Ohio, back to Kirtland, Ohio, where they lived in the Whitney Store.

- The first School of the Prophets began in the Whitney Store on January 24, 1833.

- The First Presidency was organized and empowered in the Whitney Store on March 18, 1833.

- Joseph Smith's new translation of the Bible was completed in the Whitney Store around July 2, 1833.

- Doctrine and Covenants 84–98 and 101 were all received in the Whitney Store.

Historic Kirtland: The Whitney Store

The Newel K. Whitney store was the center of many activities of the Church during the Kirtland Era and was the location where several important revelations were received. Photo by Acacia E. Griffiths.

Newel K. Whitney's early mercantile interests proved quite lucrative in Kirtland, Ohio. Making significant use of the transportation system provided by Lake Erie and the Erie Canal, Newel was able to acquire a wide variety of goods from the East Coast. In 1826, he built the two-story "White Store," a relatively large establishment for the time, on land he had purchased across the road east of his home. Newel invited his friend Sidney Gilbert to join him as a partner at N. K. Whitney and Co. The two partners kept meticulous records, and even today, visitors to their store can view a copy of their records to see whether their ancestors had been customers.

In the 1970s, the Church purchased the Whitney Store and began efforts to restore it to its original appearance. The store was dedicated by Ezra Taft Benson on August 25, 1984. A few years after, on November 18, 1988,

President Ronald Reagan gave the Church a historic preservation award for restoring the store. Today, the Whitney Store is open for tours guided by missionaries who serve at the Historic Kirtland Visitors' Center.

Visits to Kirtland

While living in Hiram, Ohio, Joseph Smith traveled to Kirtland on a few special occasions. In December 1831, he held a conference of high priests in the Whitney's home, during which the Lord revealed: "It is expedient in me for a bishop to be appointed unto you, or of you, unto the church in this part of the Lord's vineyard" (Doctrine and Covenants 72:2). Since the first bishop, Edward Partridge, had been called to Missouri, the Church was in need of another bishop in Kirtland. The Lord then indicated, "My servant Newel K. Whitney is the man who shall be appointed and ordained unto this power" (Doctrine and Covenants 72:8). Newel was humbled by this appointment, and he said to Joseph: "I cannot see a Bishop in myself, Brother Joseph; but if you say it's the Lord's will, I'll try." Joseph replied, "You need not take my word alone. Go and ask Father for yourself." As he prayed, Newel heard a voice from heaven saying, "Thy strength is in me."[22] He accepted the calling and served honorably for the rest of his life. A few months after the conference, in March, Joseph returned to the Whitneys' home to organize a business management group known as the United Firm (Doctrine and Covenants 78).

Moving Back to Kirtland from the Johnson Home in Hiram

On April 2, 1832, just a week after being tarred and feathered while living on the property of John and Elsa Johnson in Hiram, Ohio, Joseph Smith left his family to take his second trip to Missouri, as commanded by the Lord (see Doctrine and Covenants 78:9–10). Sidney Rigdon had left Hiram the day before to find temporary housing for his family in Chardon, Ohio, and later joined the Prophet on the road to Missouri. While away, Joseph wrote to his wife and asked her to move to Kirtland and stay with the Whitneys so she and

---

22   Andrew Jenson, *Latter-day Saint Biographical Encyclopedia* (Salt Lake City: Andrew Jenson History Company, 1941), 1:224.

their adopted daughter, Julia Murdock Smith, would be safe while he was gone. (Julia's twin brother, Joseph Murdock Smith, had died due to complications from being exposed to the cold night air during the tarring and feathering.)[23] Upon his return to Ohio in June, Joseph picked up his wife and daughter and returned to the Johnsons' home. It soon became clear that Hiram was no longer a safe location for the Smiths—the mobs "continued to molest and menace father Johnson's house for a long time"[24]—and that the Johnsons' home was no longer a tranquil place to continue the Bible translation. Indeed, most of the faithful Saints in the Hiram area had moved to Kirtland or Missouri. Joseph, Emma (who was seven months pregnant), and little Julia left Hiram on September 12, 1832, exactly one year after they had originally arrived.

In the meantime, Elizabeth Ann Whitney had been preparing an apartment for the Smiths on the second floor of the Whitney Store. Although it was not finished until November, the apartment was sufficiently complete to allow the Smiths to move in. This was the second time the Whitneys had provided a home for Joseph Smith and his family, and the events that occurred at this home branded it forever as one of the most sacred sites in Latter-day Saint history. Joseph received many revelations and sixteen sections of the Doctrine and Covenants in the year and a half he lived there, during which time he also completed the inspired Bible revision. The revelations were likely received in either the "translating room," which was the upstairs parlor, or the "council room," an upstairs bedroom-sized room adjacent to the parlor where the first School of the Prophets was held. The First Presidency was also formed and ordained in the Whitney Store.

Doctrine and Covenants 84: A Revelation on Priesthood

Ten days after moving back to Kirtland in 1832, the Prophet met with six recently returned elders who made "reports of their labors" (Doctrine and Covenants 84, section heading), similar to how missionaries today report to stake high councils. While meeting "together in these seasons of joy," Joseph "inquired of the Lord and received" a revelation on September 22, 1832.[25] The

---

23   Joseph Smith History, A-1, 205–209, JSP.
24   Joseph Smith History, A-1, 209, JSP.
25   Joseph Smith History, A-1, 229, JSP.

following day, in the presence of "eleven high Priests save one,"[26] Joseph received another revelation, which, after being recorded, was added to the previous one. Both revelations, now included in Doctrine and Covenants 84, were briefly described as "explaining the two priest hoods and commissioning the Apostles to preach the gospel."[27]

In this revelation, the Lord also chastised the Saints for neglecting the Book of Mormon. In the 1970s and 1980s, President Benson often quoted from Doctrine and Covenants 84 as he fulfilled the Lord's direction to emphasize the Book of Mormon (e.g., October 1986 General Conference). He particularly alluded to how the condemnation of the Missouri Saints and "the whole church" (verse 55) for not taking the Book of Mormon seriously was still applicable to the Church.

Building on previous commandments to proclaim the gospel (see Doctrine and Covenants 42:6, 12), the Lord also gave an extensive set of instructions regarding how he wanted missionary work to be carried out in this dispensation. He explained that it was God's high priests' responsibility to serve missions (verse 32), that those priests were to bear "testimony to all the world of those things which [were] communicated unto [them]" (verse 63), that those who received the priests should "feed . . . clothe . . . and give [them] money" (verse 89) while they served without "purse or scrip" (verse 78), and that dire consequences would result from rejecting the priests' message. The editors of The Joseph Smith Papers suggested that "this revelation seemed to launch a more urgent and comprehensive missionary campaign, even including in its preaching assignments individuals such as Bishop Newel K. Whitney, who generally oversaw temporal, not spiritual, concerns."[28]

Doctrine and Covenants 85: A Revealed Letter to W. W. Phelps

In early October 1832, shortly after receiving the revelations now found in Doctrine and Covenants 84, Joseph Smith and Newel K. Whitney traveled to New York to proselyte and to acquire merchandise. They arrived back in Kirtland on November 6, just a few hours after Emma gave birth to the first of her four biological children that would live to adulthood, a child they named Joseph Smith III. On the November 27, the Prophet composed a letter

---

26   Joseph Smith History, A-1, 229, JSP.
27   Revelation Book 2, Index, [1], JSP.
28   "Historical Introduction," Revelation, September 22–23, 1832 [D&C 84], JSP.

to William W. Phelps. This letter contained revelation concerning what to do about the Saints who had traveled to Zion in Jackson County, Missouri, but had failed to comply with the commandment to consecrate their properties to the Church. The gathering to Zion was to be an orderly endeavor, "not in haste, lest there be confusion" (Doctrine and Covenants 63:24; see also 58:56) and directed by the Prophet, whom the Lord would give "power that he shall be enabled to discern by the Spirit those who shall go up unto the land of Zion, and those of [the Lord's] disciples who shall tarry" (Doctrine and Covenants 63:41). However, many Saints migrated there without permission and, as indicated, had not consecrated their properties, both of which complications placed an undue burden upon the local economy. Indeed, that burden was among the factors that led Missouri residents to disapprove of the migrating Saints.

Doctrine and Covenants 86: An Inspired Interpretation of the Wheat and Tares Parable

An example of good sold in the Whitney Store. Photo by Acacia E. Griffiths.

Nine days after receiving the revelation now found in Doctrine and Covenants 85, the Prophet received a revelation while he was reviewing and editing the manuscript for his new translation of the Bible. The revelation, now Doctrine and Covenants 86, provided an inspired interpretation of the Savior's parable of the wheat and the tares (see Matthew 13). Joseph had finished the initial translation of the New Testament in early July 1832 but then commenced a revision of that work while also translating the Old Testament. His initial translation of the parable the year earlier had resulted in a few substantive changes, but while reviewing the thirtieth verse this second time, he changed the order of the gathering. In the King James Version, it says, "I will say to the reapers, gather ye together first the tares" (Matthew 13:30); in Joseph's inspired revision, it says, "Gather ye together first the wheat into my barn; and the tares are bound in bundles to be burned"(Matthew 13:29). Section 86 likewise reads, "First gather out the wheat" (verse 7).

The last three verses of Doctrine and Covenants 86 provides an incredible explication of the role of the Abrahamic covenant in our Father's plan of salvation. Verse 8 states, "Therefore, thus saith the Lord unto you, with whom the priesthood hath continued through the lineage of your fathers." Of this verse, Elder Theodore M. Burton explained: "In this scripture the Lord was not talking about your priesthood line of authority. He was talking about your inherited right to receive and use priesthood power. This readiness to listen and believe is an inherited gift which enabled you to recognize and accept the truth. . . . This means we receive a right to priesthood blessings from our blood ancestry."[29]

29   Theodore M. Burton, "Salvation for the Dead—A Missionary Activity," *Ensign*, May 1975.

Doctrine and Covenants 87: Prophecy on War

The table in the translation room in the Whitney Store. Several key revelations, including the "Revelation on War" (Doctrine and Covenants 87), and the "Olive Leaf" (Doctrine and Covenants 88) were received here.

In his history, Joseph Smith wrote about the serious disagreements in the United States regarding how much control national government should have over individual states: "Appearances of troubles among the nations, became more visible, this season, than they had previously done, since the church began her journey out of the wilderness."[30] South Carolina had passed an ordinance declaring that national tariff laws were unconstitutional, and the people of that state prepared for military action against the federal government. Joseph added, "The United States, amid all her pomp and greatness, was threatened with immediate dissolution. The people of South Carolina, in convention assembled, (in November,) passed ordinances, declaring their state, a free and Independent Nation. . . . President [Andrew] Jackson issued his proclamation against this rebellion; called out a force sufficient to quell it, and implored the blessings of God to assist the Nation to extricate itself from the horrors of the approaching and Solemn Crisis." Joseph then wrote that he received a revelation—a prophecy of war—on Christmas Day of 1832.[31] Thankfully, a new tariff law was passed in March 1833 that represented a compromise between northern and southern perspectives, temporarily preventing civil war at that time. However, Joseph reiterated some aspects of this prophecy relating specifically to an American civil war in Nauvoo in 1843: "I prophesy, in the

30   Joseph Smith History, A-1, 244, JSP.
31   Joseph Smith History, A-1, 244, JSP.

name of the Lord God, that the commencement of the difficulties which will cause much bloodshed previous to the coming of the Son of Man will be in South Carolina. It may probably arise through the slave question. This a voice declared to me, while I was praying earnestly on the subject, December 25th, 1832" (Doctrine and Covenants 130:12–13).

Despite staving off the potential bloodshed for a time, the tariff law only postponed the fulfillment of some aspects of Joseph's prophecy, which is sometimes called the Civil War prophecy. But the prophecy predicts much more than the American Civil War. All in all, the details of every aspect of the prophecy have been and continue to be fulfilled.

Doctrine and Covenants 88: The Olive Leaf

Joseph Smith called the revelation now found in Doctrine and Covenants 88 the "'olive leaf' . . . plucked from the Tree of Paradise, the Lord's message of peace to us" (Doctrine and Covenants 88, section heading). In modern vernacular, we would probably call this revelation an "olive branch" because Joseph sent it to Zion to help mend feelings of disunity and contention. As the Lord suggested in Doctrine and Covenants 84:76, "Your brethren in Zion" were to be "upbraided . . . for their rebellion against you." Joseph further commented on the rebellion: "Though our brethren in Zion indulge in feelings towards us, which are not according to the requirements of the new covenant, yet we have the satisfaction of knowing that the Lord approves of us and has accepted us, and established his name in Kirtland for the salvation of the nations. . . . For if Zion, will not purify herself . . . he will seek another people. . . . Repent, repent, is the voice of God to Zion."[32] What were the Saints in Zion guilty of? In addition to issues around the law of consecration already discussed in this chapter, many Saints were ignoring the authority of local leaders to preside, charging Joseph with "seeking after Monarchal power and authority," and accusing Joseph of purposely putting off settling in Zion.[33]

After the Saints received section 88, Orson Hyde and Hyrum Smith were assigned to write a letter of chastisement to the leadership in Zion. They wrote: "We therefore, Orson and Hyrum, the committee appointed by said conference to write this epistle, having received the prayers of said conference that we might be enabled to write the mind and will of God upon this subject, now

32   Joseph Smith to William W. Phelps, January 11, 1833, JSP.
33   Orson Hyde and Hyrum Smith to Edward Partridge, January 14, 1833, JSP.

take up our pen to address you in the name of the conference, relying upon the arm of the Great Head of the Church." Then, paraphrasing Doctrine and Covenants 84:56–59, they alluded to some temporary resolutions which had no long-term effect: "At the time Joseph, Sidney, and Newel left Zion [in June 1832], all matters of hardness and misunderstanding were settled and buried (as they supposed), and you gave them the hand of fellowship, but afterwards you brought up all these things again in a censorious spirit, accusing Brother Joseph in rather an indirect way of seeking after monarchal power and authority. This came to us in Brother Corrill's letter of June 2nd."[34]

Fortunately, these communications between the two groups of Saints seemed to create the desired effect. In a high priest council held in Zion on February 26, 1833, the five Zion branches were assigned to hold solemn assemblies "as a day of confession, and repentance."[35] Then Oliver Cowdery, William W. Phelps, and John Corrill sent a letter to Joseph on behalf of the Saints in Zion, expressing the Saints' desire to keep the commandments in the future. This result was the reason the Lord said "the angels rejoice over [the Saints in Missouri]" (Doctrine and Covenants 90:34).

Frederick G. Williams, Joseph Smith's second counselor in the First Presidency, described how the Prophet prepared those who were with him in the Whitney Store to receive revelation:

> Brother Joseph arose and said, to receive revelation and the blessings of heaven, it was necessary to have our minds on God and exercise faith and become of one heart and of one mind; therefore, he recommended all present to pray separately and vocally. . . . Accordingly, we all bowed down before the Lord, after which each one arose and spoke in his turn his feelings, . . . and then proceeded to receive a revelation. . . . The revelation not being finished, the conference adjourned. . . .
>
> [The meeting] commenced by prayer then proceeded to receive the residue of the above revelation.[36]

After the participants prayed, Joseph received the revelation now contained in Doctrine and Covenants 88. The revelations, given over two days, included instructions to the Prophet about preparing the Saints for to receive sacred covenants. He told the missionaries in Kirtland to "call [their] solemn

---

34   Orson Hyde and Hyrum Smith to Edward Partridge, January 14, 1833, JSP.
35   David Pettegrew, Journal, 1840–1857, 1926–1930, 15, MS 22278, Church History Library, Salt Lake City.
36   Minutes, December 27–28, 1832, 3–4, JSP.

assembly, as [he has] commanded [them]" (verse 117), indeed to "tarry in this place" in order prepare for a "solemn assembly" (verse 70) by doing five things:

1. "Organize yourselves" (verses 74, 119). This commandment was accomplished when Joseph organized priesthood holders into quorums with quorum presidencies (see also Doctrine and Covenants 107).

2. "Sanctify yourselves; yea, purify your hearts, and cleanse your hands and your feet before me, that I may make you clean" (verse 74). "Abide ye in the liberty wherewith ye are made free; entangle not yourselves in sin, but let your hands be clean" (verse 86). This instruction became a consistent emphasis of the Prophet in his preaching and exhortations.

3. "Teach one another the doctrine of the kingdom. Teach ye diligently and my grace shall attend you, that you may be instructed . . . in the law of the gospel . . . of things both in heaven and in the earth, and under the earth; things which have been, things which are, things which must shortly come to pass; things which are at home, things which are abroad" (verses 77–79). "Seek ye diligently and teach one another words of wisdom" (verse 118). "Appoint among yourselves a teacher, and let not all be spokesmen at once; but let one speak at a time and let all listen unto his sayings" (verse 122). The School of the Prophets was first held in the Whitney Store, then later in the printing house next to the temple, and finally in the temple itself, where the school was also called "the school of mine apostles" (Doctrine and Covenants 95:17; see also 90:7; 95:10; 97:3).

4. "See that ye love one another; cease to be covetous; learn to impart one to another as the gospel requires. . . . Cease to find fault one with another. . . . Clothe yourselves with the bond of charity, as with a mantle, which is the bond of perfectness and peace (verses 123–125). This instruction was another consistent emphasis, particularly among the leadership of the Church.

5. "Establish a house, even a house of prayer, a house of fasting, a house of faith, a house of learning, a house of glory, a house of order, a house of God" (verse 119). Interestingly, from verses 117 to the end of the section, the Lord intermingled his commands to establish a school and to build a temple. For example, verses 129 and 130 tell what the teacher should do when entering the school in the "house of God." Likewise, in verse 137 the Lord said: "In all your doings in the house of the Lord, in the school of the prophets." As the historical record indicates, the first location of the school was temple-like because there they performed ordinances, washed feet (verse 139), and the Father

and the Son were seen walking among them, as described in the section on Doctrine and Covenants 90 in this chapter. Similarly, in the second location of the school—the printing house—the washing ordinance was performed, and the third location of the school was actually on the second floor of the temple.

Doctrine and Covenants 89: A Word of Wisdom

The School of the Prophets room in the Whitney Store. This small, unventilated room played a key role in the reception of the Word of Wisdom (Doctrine and Covenants 89). Photo by Acacia E. Griffiths.

In 1822, the culture in the United States (and elsewhere) was intricately intertwined with the use of substances that Latter-day Saints now recognize as forbidden. Men, women, and children consumed alcohol in the form of fermented, distilled, or brewed drinks three times a day on average, with consumption totaling twenty gallons per person per year. Sponsoring a cultural activity of any kind without serving alcohol was unthinkable, and as such, one writer chose the title *The Alcoholic Republic* for a book about the United States. The term *hot drinks* was widely used to refer to coffee and tea, and men, women, and children were known to drink them three times a day as well. (There are many types of teas, and the Church has clarified that the type referred to in the Word of Wisdom is commonly known as *green tea* or *black tea*, both of which come from the same type of plant.[37]) Large amounts of meat were also eaten with the same regularity. Chewing or smoking tobacco was viewed as "good for what ails ya," touted to cure anything from asthma to flatulence. Chewers didn't hesitate to spew, no matter where they found themselves—even if they happened to be in someone's home and no spittoon was available.

Brigham Young, though not a direct witness of the revelation of the Word of Wisdom, described the circumstances surrounding it:

> The first school of the prophets was held in a small room [eleven by fourteen] situated over the Prophet Joseph's kitchen, in a house which belonged to Bishop Whitney. . . . The brethren came to that place for hundreds of miles to attend school in a little room. . . . When they assembled together in this room after breakfast, the first they did was to light their pipes, and, while smoking, talk about the great things of the kingdom, and spit all over the room, and as soon as the pipe was out of their mouths a large chew of tobacco would then be taken. Often when the Prophet [Joseph Smith] entered the room to give the school instructions he would find himself in a cloud of tobacco smoke. This, and the complaints of his wife at having to clean so filthy a floor, made the Prophet think upon the matter, and he inquired of the Lord relating to the conduct of the Elders in using tobacco, and the revelation known as the Word of Wisdom was the result of his inquiry.[38]

Joseph Smith received the revelation in the presence of two or three brethren in the parlor room next to where the school was held. In attendance at the school were Joseph Smith, Hyrum Smith, William Smith, Frederick G. Williams, Orson Hyde (who had the charge of the school), Zebedee Coltrin, Sylvester Smith, Joseph Smith Sr., Levi Hancock, Martin Harris, Sidney Rigdon, Newel K. Whitney, Samuel H. Smith, John Murdock, Lyman Johnson, and Ezra Thayer. Zebedee, an eventual President of the Seventy, described what happened after Joseph presented the revelation to the school: "When the Word of Wisdom was first presented by the Prophet Joseph Smith (as he came out of the translating room) . . . , there were twenty out of the

---

37   "Vaping, Coffee, Tea, and Marijuana," *New Era*, August 2019.
38   Brigham Young, "School of the Prophets—Improvement of Provo City—Litigation—Injudicious Trading," *Journal of Discourses* (Liverpool, 1869), 12:158, https://contentdm.lib.byu.edu/digital/collection/JournalOfDiscourses3/id/9838.

twenty-one who used tobacco and they all immediately threw their tobacco and pipes into the fire."[39] (Recent archeological findings have revealed old pipes in the fireplace's original location.[40]) Zebedee also commented on how these brethren were able to demonstrate immediate obedience: "Those who gave up using tobacco eased off on licorice root, but there was no easing off on tea and coffee; these they had to give up straight off or their fellowship was jeopardized."[41]

The Lord himself called this revelation found in section 89 "A WORD OF WISDOM" (verse 1) and communicated his expectations relative to obeying it, saying: "To be sent greeting; not by commandment or constraint, but by revelation and the word of wisdom" (verse 2). About the Lord's expectations, Joseph F. Smith explained: "The reason undoubtedly why the Word of Wisdom was given—as not by 'commandment or constraint' was that at that time, at least, if it had been given as a commandment it would have brought every man, addicted to the use of these noxious things, under condemnation; so the Lord was merciful and gave them a chance to overcome, before He brought them under the law."[42]

39   School of the Prophets Salt Lake City meeting minutes, October 3, 1883, CR 390 5, Church History Library, Salt Lake City.

40   Mark Lyman Staker, *Hearken O Ye People: The Historical Setting of Joseph Smith's Ohio Revelations* (Salt Lake City, Utah, 2010).

41   School of the Prophets Salt Lake City meeting minutes, October 11, 1883, CR 390 5, Church History Library, Salt Lake City.

42   Joseph F. Smith, *Eighty-Fourth Semi-Annual Conference of The Church of Jesus Christ of Latter-day Saints* (Salt Lake City: Deseret News, 1913), 14, https://archive.org/details/conferencereport1913sa/page/n15/mode/2up.

Doctrine and Covenants 90: The First Presidency

The School of the Prophets room in the Whitney Store. This small, unventilated room played a key role in the reception of the Word of Wisdom (Doctrine and Covenants 89). Photo by Acacia E. Griffiths.

There is no extant historical record that provides the immediate context for the revelation contained in Doctrine and Covenants 90. However, the heading states, "This revelation is a continuing step in the establishment of the First Presidency." Although beyond the purview of this chapter, those steps tell of a remarkable series of revelations and events attesting to the divinity of the on-going restoration of the gospel and the organization of the Church.

In an unpublished revelation received in March 1832, the Lord revealed that the Prophet should have counselors. "Unto the office of the presidency of the high Priesthood I have given authority to preside with the assistance of his councellers over all the Concerns of the church."[43] In another unpublished revelation given in that same month, the Lord called for the selection and ordination of Jesse Gause and Sidney Rigdon as "councillers of the ministry of the presidency of the high Pristhood."[44]

In a revelation originally provided for Jesse Gause, the Lord said: "Hearken to the calling wherewith you are called, even to be a high priest in my church, and a counselor unto my servant Joseph Smith, Jun.; Unto whom I have given the keys of the kingdom, which belong always unto the Presidency of the High Priesthood" (Doctrine and Covenants 81:1–2). The current version of section

---

43   Revelation, between circa 8 and circa 24 March 1832, JSP.
44   Note, 8 March 1832, 11, JSP.

81 uses the name of Frederick G. Williams rather than Jesse, and the heading to that section explains the reasoning behind the revision:

> The historical records show that when this revelation was received in March 1832, it called Jesse Gause to the office of counselor to Joseph Smith in the Presidency. However, when he failed to continue in a manner consistent with this appointment, the call was subsequently transferred to Frederick G. Williams. The revelation (dated March 1832) should be regarded as a step toward the formal organization of the First Presidency, specifically calling for the office of counselor in that body and explaining the dignity of the appointment. Brother Gause served for a time but was excommunicated from the Church in December 1832.

In March 1833 the Lord revealed, "And again, verily I say unto thy brethren, Sidney Rigdon and Frederick G. Williams, their sins are forgiven them also, and they are accounted as equal with thee in holding the keys of this last kingdom" (Doctrine and Covenants 90:6). The heading to section 90 explains, "This revelation is a continuing step in the establishment of the First Presidency (see the heading to section 81); as a consequence thereof, the counselors mentioned were ordained on March 18, 1833." The counselors' ordination took place in the School of the Prophets in the Whitney Store at the behest of Sidney. In a continuation of divine manifestations in Ohio that began on the Morley Farm and continued in Hiram, the Father and the Son were seen in conjunction with this milestone day in restoration history. Joseph stated:

> I exhorted the brethren to faithfulness and diligence in keeping the commandments of God, and gave much instruction for the benefit of the Saints, with a promise that the pure in heart should see a heavenly vision; and after remaining a short time in secret prayer, the promise was verified; for many present had the eyes of their understanding opened by the Spirit of God, so as to behold many things. . . . Many of the brethren saw a heavenly vision of the Savior, and concourses of angels, and many other things, of which each one has a record of what he saw."[45]

Zebedee Coltrin, a participant in the proceedings of that day, recounted the following:

---

45   Joseph Smith, *History of the Church*, ed. B. H. Roberts (Salt Lake City: Deseret Book Company, 1948), 1:334,.

At one of these meetings after the organization of the school, on the 23rd of January, 1833, when we were all together, Joseph having given instructions, and while engaged in silent prayer, kneeling, with our hands uplifted each one praying in silence, no one whispered above his breath, a personage walked through the room from east to west, and Joseph asked if we saw him. I saw him and suppose the others did and Joseph answered, "that is Jesus, the Son of God, our elder brother." Afterwards Joseph told us to resume our former position in prayer, which we did. Another person came through; he was surrounded as with a flame of fire. [I] experienced a sensation that it might destroy the tabernacle as it was of consuming fire of great brightness. The Prophet Joseph said this was the Father of our Lord Jesus Christ. I saw Him.[46]

Section 90 also contains one of only two revelations directed specifically to a Latter-day Saint woman. The Lord revealed his will for Vienna Jaques: "My handmaid Vienna Jaques should receive money to bear her expenses, and go up unto the land of Zion" (verse 28). The Lord was blessing her for her willingness to obey the command that "the residue of [her] money [a sum of $1,400] may be consecrated unto [him]" (verse 29). She then received assistance that enabled her to "go up unto the land of Zion, and receive an inheritance from the hand of the bishop" (verse 30). She was also promised that "she may settle down in peace inasmuch as she is faithful" (verse 31), but she would be "rewarded in [the Lord's] own due time" (verse 29). First, she endured the expulsion of the Saints from Jackson County in November 1833, aided the sick of Zion's Camp in 1834, suffered another expulsion of the Saints from the state of Missouri in 1839, settled in Nauvoo in 1842, drove a wagon at age sixty across the plains with the Charles C. Rich Company, arrived in the Salt Lake Valley on October 2, 1847, and lived in her wagon for a year before receiving a lot in the Salt Lake 12th Ward. There, she lived faithfully until her death at age ninety-six.

---

46   School of the Prophets Salt Lake City meeting minutes, October 3, 1883, CR 390 5, Church History Library, Salt Lake City.

Doctrine Covenants 91 and 92:
Two Short Revelations

During his time living above the Whitney Store and nearing the end of his Bible translation work in March 1833, the Prophet sought the guidance of the Lord about whether his translation should include the Apocrypha. The apocrypha consists of a set of books included in Catholic Bibles but generally excluded from Protestant ones. The Lord replied, "There are many things contained therein that are true, and it is mostly translated correctly," but "there are many things contained therein that are not true, which are interpolations by the hands of men" (Doctrine and Covenants 91:1–2). Therefore, it was "not needful that the Apocrypha should be translated" (verse 3). However, "whoso readeth it . . . [and] is enlightened by the Spirit shall obtain benefit therefrom" (verses 4–5).

That same month, Frederick G. Williams, who was recently called as the Second Counselor in the First Presidency, was directed by revelation to be received into the newly organized United Firm. The Lord promised him, "Inasmuch as you are faithful in keeping all former commandments you shall be blessed forever" (Doctrine and Covenants 92:2). Except for a brief time during which he lost his position and his Church membership (over difficulties associated with the failure of the Kirtland Safety Society), Frederick was faithful to the end of his life.

Doctrine and Covenants 93:
The Record of John the Baptist

A shelf of goods in the Whitney Store. Photo by Acacia E. Griffiths.

The Prophet received the revelation now found in Doctrine and Covenants 93 on May 6, 1833. There is very little historical background surrounding this revelation. Perhaps one way to contextualize section 93 is to refer back to section 90, in which Joseph was directed to continue his translation of the Old Testament and "from time to time, as shall be manifested by the Comforter, receive revelations to unfold the mysteries of the kingdom" (verse 14). If there were ever a revelation that unfolded the mysteries, it would be section 93. However, one of the compilers of The Joseph Smith Papers wrote the following regarding this section: "The text of the revelation appears to be closely related to the first chapter of the Gospel according to John but was likely not the direct result of [Joseph's] work revising the New Testament, since the revision had been completed three months earlier, on 2 February 1833. Further, the revisions to John's record made in this revelation generally vary from the changes [Joseph] made to the same text in his larger project of revising the Bible."[47]

In spite of what is lacking, we do know something of the section's extraordinary source, and remarkably, the revelation itself describes it by making a

---

47   "Historical Introduction," Revelation, May 6, 1833, JSP.

different sort of connection to John's Gospel. Verse 6 reads, "And John saw and bore record of the fulness of my glory, and the fulness of John's record is hereafter to be revealed." The Lord doesn't directly identify who this John is, but it's natural to think he is referring to John the Apostle. In fact, as stated in the previous paragraph, the teachings in section 93 are closely related to John chapter 1 in the New Testament; however, John himself suggests that that chapter is taken from a record kept by another John, even John the Baptist. He wrote, "This is the record of John, when the Jews sent priests and Levites from Jerusalem to ask him, Who art thou? . . . He said, I am the voice of one crying in the wilderness" (John 1:19, 23). Elder Bruce R. McConkie validates this conclusion:

> From latter-day revelation we learn that the material in the forepart of the gospel of John (the Apostle, Revelator, and Beloved Disciple) was written originally by John the Baptist. By revelation the Lord restored to Joseph Smith part of what John the Baptist had written and promised to reveal the balance when men became sufficiently faithful to warrant receiving it. . . . Even without revelation, however, it should be evident that John the Baptist had something to do with the recording of events in the forepart of John's gospel, for some of the occurrences include his conversations with the Jews and a record of what he saw when our Lord was baptized—all of which matters would have been unknown to John the Apostle whose ministry began somewhat later than that of the Baptist's. There is little doubt but that the Beloved Disciple had before him the Baptist's account when he wrote his gospel. The latter John either copied or paraphrased what the earlier prophet of the same name had written.[48]

A close inspection of Doctrine and Covenants 93:15 suggests that the account of John the Baptist may have been revealed to John the Apostle, at least in part, at the time John the Baptist baptized Jesus: "And I, John, bear record, and lo, the heavens were opened, and the Holy Ghost descended upon him in the form of a dove, and sat upon him, and there came a voice out of heaven saying: This is my beloved Son."

---

48   Bruce R. McConkie, *Doctrinal New Testament Commentary*, vol. 1, *The Gospels* (Salt Lake City: Bookcraft, 1965), 70–71; see also Bruce R. McConkie, *The Mortal Messiah*, vol. 1, *From Bethlehem to Calvary* (Salt Lake City, Deseret Book Company, 1979), 426–27.

Doctrine and Covenants 94, 95, and 96: The Kirtland Temple

The Kirtland Temple at dusk. Photo by Casey Paul Griffiths.

Despite the large time commitment required to participate in the School of the Prophets, some efforts were made to prepare for building a temple. In the spring of 1833, leaders negotiated for the Peter French Farm, upon which they designated an area to build the temple. They also purchased sixteen acres of heavily forested timber land to provide lumber for the temple. At a high priests' conference at the Whitney Store on May 4, 1833, participants appointed a building and donation committee: Reynolds Cahoon, Jared Carter, and Hyrum Smith. However, the council may have been confused about the distinction between a school (a building for educational purposes) and a temple (a building for worship) because the committee seemed to be primarily focused on building an educational facility out of logs. To the latter proposal, Joseph replied: "Shall we brethren build a house for Our God, of logs? No brethren I have a better plan than that I have the plan of the house of the Lord given by himself, [and] you will see by this the difference between our calculations and his Ideas."[49]

---

49   Lucy Mack Smith, History, 1844–1845, bk. 14 [1], JSP.

The Lord himself also expressed his displeasure with the committee's focus. On June 1, 1833,[50] in another high priests' conference, he said: "Ye have sinned against me a very grievous sin, in that ye have not considered the great commandment in all things, that I have given unto you concerning the building of mine house" (Doctrine and Covenants 95:3). He directed that the temple would have an outer court and an inner court, and that the size of the inner court was to be "fifty and five feet in width, and let it be sixty-five feet in length" (verse 15). He said, "Let the lower part of the inner court be dedicated unto me for your sacrament offering, and for your preaching, and your fasting, and your praying, and the offering up of your most holy desires unto me. . . . And let the higher part of the inner court be dedicated unto me for the school of mine apostles" (verses 16–17). He also directed, "Let it be built after the manner which I shall show unto three of you, whom ye shall appoint and ordain unto this power" (verse 14). A few days later, Frederick G. Williams recounted that the First Presidency "'went upon [their] knees, called on the Lord, and the building appeared within viewing distance.'" He further explained, "'I [was] the first to discover it. Then all of us viewed it together. After we had taken a good look at the exterior, the building seemed to come right over us; and the makeup of this Hall seems to coincide with what I there saw to a minutia.'"[51] Shortly thereafter, Frederick drew architectural plans based on this revelation.

On June 6, another conference of high priests assigned the same three original school building committee members, Hyrum Smith, Jared Carter, and Reynolds Cahoon, to oversee temple construction. On June 7, Hyrum recorded the following in his diary: "This Day Commenced making Preparation for the Building the House of the Lord."[52] He also wrote, "We are preparing to build a house for the Lord and I am determined to be the first at the work."[53] He apparently ran to the building site and used a scythe to cut down the Smith family wheat crop that was growing there. His mother also recorded, "Hyrum

---

50   The dating for this meeting and accompanying revelation is somewhat uncertain. There is some evidence that it may have happened on June 4 or that portions of these events occurred on both June 1 and June 4. See Minutes, circa 1 June 1833, JSP.

51   Truman O. Angell, Autobiography, 1884, MS 12334, 14–15, Church History Library, Salt Lake City.

52   Hyrum Smith, Diary, June 7, 1833, MS 2945, Church History Library, Salt Lake City; there is some confusion in the historical records as to the actual date construction commenced.

53   Lucy Mack Smith, History, 1844–1845, bk. 14, [1–2], JSP.

commenced digging a trench for the wall, he having declared that he would strike the first blow upon the house."[54]

Three days later, during a high priest conference on June 4, "the chief subject of consideration was the disposal of certain lands, known as the French farm, possessed by the Church near Kirtland. Since the conference could not agree who should take charge of the farm, all agreed to inquire of the Lord concerning the matter" (Doctrine and Covenants 96, section heading). The Lord had already directed that the temple be built on the farm, but now these brethren wanted to know what to do with the rest of the property, which included a tavern, a brick kiln, and several acres of land. The heading of section 96 also says this revelation was "an example to the Saints in Kirtland." This simple phrase may have at least two meanings. First, the revelation may have been meant to show the Saints how to establish a "stake that [the Lord had] set for the strength of Zion [to] be made strong" (verse 1). During Joseph Smith's time, and later in Utah, the establishment of stakes always included the building of cities and the providing of inheritances within those cities as stewardships according to the law of consecration. Thus the Lord said, "Let it be divided into lots, according to wisdom, for the benefit of those who seek inheritances, as it shall be determined in council among you" (verse 3). Another way the revelation may have served as an example to the Kirtland Saints is in the process that brought about the revelation: the brethren could not reach consensus on a matter of importance, so they sought the Lord's guidance. Furthermore, the directions provided in the revelation were carried out immediately; on the same day they received the revelation, they assigned Newel K. Whitney to manage the French Farm (verse 2) and admitted John Johnson to the United Firm (verses 6–9).

Prior to this revelation, the Church's printing press had been in the Johnson Inn on the French Farm, but in this revelation, the Lord also instructed the Saints to build a new printing house: "Therefore, take heed that ye see to this matter, and that portion that is necessary to benefit mine order, for the purpose of bringing forth my word to the children of men. For behold, verily I say unto you, this is the most expedient in me, that my word should go forth unto the children of men, for the purpose of subduing the hearts of the children of men for your good" (Doctrine and Covenants 96:4–5). While the temple was under construction, the Saints built the two-story printing house next to the northwest corner of the temple. This new printing house also served as

54   Lucy Smith, *Biographical Sketches of Joseph Smith, the Prophet, and His Progenitors for Many Generations* (Liverpool, 1853), 203.

the second location for the School of the Prophets and, thus, the location for the printing of the Lectures on Faith. It also served as an office space for the First Presidency and as the first location for the initiatory washings associated with the temple endowment.

On August 2, 1833, two months after the printing house was constructed, the Lord directed two more temples be built according to the same specifications as revealed in section 95—one "for the work of the presidency, in obtaining revelations; and for the work of the ministry of the presidency, in all things pertaining to the church and kingdom" and another "for the work of the printing of the translation of my scriptures, and all things whatsoever I shall command you" (Doctrine and Covenants 94:3, 10). He added, "These two houses are not to be built until I give unto you a commandment concerning them" (verse 16). It is yet possible that the Lord intends for these temples to be built. He continues to fulfill his promise to "build up Kirtland" (Doctrine and Covenants 124:83).

Doctrine and Covenants 97, 98, and 101: Revelation Amid Persecution

Exterior of the Whitney Store. Photo by Acacia E. Griffiths.

The Lord commanded Joseph Smith to travel to Jackson County, Missouri, in June 1831 with a large company of missionary companionships. Joseph was told that when the company arrived there, the location of Zion, the New Jerusalem, "would be made known unto them" (Doctrine and Covenants 52:5). Upon arriving in Jackson County in July, the Lord said: "This is the land of promise, and the place for the city of Zion" (Doctrine and Covenants 57:2). Thus began the gathering to Zion, and in effect, the designation of two gathering places: Jackson County and Kirtland. The first to be directed to gather in Jackson County were the Saints from Colesville, New York (Doctrine and Covenants 54), and a few other specific families, including the families of William W. Phelps, Edward Partridge, and Sidney Gilbert (Doctrine and Covenants 55; 57).

By the time sections 97, 98, and 101 were revealed, at least 1,200 Saints had gathered to Zion in five settlements, or branches. When the gathering began, there was peace and prosperity, but that didn't last for long. Contentions between the Saints and the other Missouri settlers arose due to a number of factors, which included differences in perspectives about black slavery, suspicions of the Saints stirring up the Indians, jealousy on the part of the leaders of other churches, doctrinal differences, local citizens' fears that the Saints would gain political control because of their large numbers, strains placed on the economy by the relative poverty of many of those who gathered (which was partly because many more Saints moved there than were approved by the Prophet; see Doctrine and Covenants 63:41), and the tendency of some Saints to make the local citizens nervous by telling them that God had given their land to the Saints.

Random acts of mob violence commenced in the fall of 1832 and came to a head on July 23, 1833, when Edward Partridge and Charles Allen were tarred and feathered and the printing shop of William W. Phelps was ransacked and its printing press destroyed. The Missouri Church leaders agreed to leave Jackson County; half of the Saints were to leave by January 1, 1834, and the other half by the following April 1.

Shortly before this violence, two letters were sent from leaders of the Church in Missouri—one from the leaders of the School of the Prophets and one from Oliver Cowdery. These letters prompted the First Presidency to reply on August 7 with a lengthy letter to Edward Partridge containing three revelations that now appear in Doctrine and Covenants 94, 97, and 98. Although the content of the letters from Missouri is unknown, the revelations contained in the reply, along with the reply itself, suggest that the Missouri leaders wanted guidance about printing, the School of the Prophets, and mob aggression against the Saints.

Mini-Devotional—The Process of Revelation

Frederick G. Williams recorded that the Prophet Joseph Smith[55] invited others to engage in the following process preparatory to receiving revelation:

- have your mind on God
- exercise faith
- become of one heart and of one mind
- pray separately and vocally

Consider a question or problem for which you could use divine help—either an individual matter or one involving others. Follow Joseph's outlined process to see whether doing so helps you learn to "Hear Him."[56]

---

55   Minutes, December 27–28, 1832, 3–4, JSP.

56   President Russell M. Nelson, *Invitation from the Prophet: Hear Him*, The Church of Jesus Christ of Latter-day Saints, accessed July 23, 2022, https://www.churchofjesuschrist.org/study/manual/hear-him-launch/hear-him?lang=eng.

Significant events at this location:

- In the fall of 1830, Oliver Cowdery, Parley P. Pratt, Ziba Peterson, and Peter Whitmer Jr., who were called to preach to the Lamanites, arrived in the Kirtland area.

- In February 1831, Joseph and Emma Smith moved to Kirtland, Ohio, and stayed in the home of Newel K. and Elizabeth Ann Whitney for a few weeks.

- On February 4, 1831, the Lord called Edward Partridge as the first bishop of the Church (see Doctrine and Covenants 41).

- On February 9 and 23, the Lord revealed "the Law," which he had promised would be given in Ohio (see Doctrine and Covenants 42).

- In March 1831, Joseph Smith healed the lame arm of Elsa Johnson.

- On December 4, 1831, Newel K. Whitney was called as the second bishop of the Church (see Doctrine and Covenants 72).

- In January 1836, the Whitney family held a "feast for the poor."

- Doctrine and Covenants 41, 42, 43 and 44 were all received while Joseph and Emma Smith were staying in the Whitney home.

Historic Kirtland: The Newel K. and Elizabeth Ann Whitney Home

The home of Newel K. and Elizabeth Ann Whitney at the Kirtland Historic Site. Photo by Acacia E. Griffiths.

In February 1831, Joseph and Emma Smith arrived in Kirtland, obedient to the Lord's command to gather to Ohio. Newel K. and Elizabeth Ann Whitney opened their home to the Smiths, and in doing so, it became an important part of Church history. During the few short weeks that the Prophet lived with the Whitneys, he received four revelations. In two of these, the Lord called the first bishop of the Church and revealed "the Law" as well as the beginnings of the law of consecration. In this same house, Joseph performed one of the first recorded priesthood healings of this dispensation when he healed Elsa Johnson's lame arm. Even after Joseph and Emma moved away, the Whitney home continued to serve as a place of gathering for the Saints and as a place of refuge for the poor and needy in the surrounding area. Most importantly, this house served as the home to the Whitney family, whose faith, devotion, and sacrifice serve as an enduring example.

Newel K. and Elizabeth Ann Whitney

Newel Kimball Whitney was born February 5, 1795, in Marlborough, Vermont. He was the first son and second child of Samuel Whitney and Susannah Kimball. At age nineteen, he opened a merchandising business selling supplies to the United States army during the War of 1812. During one of the final skirmishes of the war, Newel lost all his property. He then began trading with Native Americans around Lake Michigan and the Great Lakes. He soon met Sidney Gilbert, who had opened a store in Mentor, Ohio. He asked Newel to be one of his store clerks.

Elizabeth Ann Smith was born December 26, 1800, in Derby, Connecticut. She was the oldest child of Gibson Smith and Polly Bradley. She was well educated as a child, and when she turned eighteen years old, she moved to Ohio with her aunt Sarah Smith. Sarah purchased a piece of property near Kirtland, Ohio, and these two single women sought to make a life for themselves.

Within a few months of moving to the Kirtland area, Ann (her preferred name) met Newel as he passed through the area on a business trip. Of that encounter Ann wrote, "In [Newel's] travels to and from New York he passed through the country where we resided, and 'we met by chance,' became attached to each other, and my aunt granting her full approval, we were married after a courtship of reasonable length."[57] They courted for three years, and during that time, Newel moved to Kirtland and opened his own store. Ann and Newel were married on October 20, 1822. Ann recalled, "Ours was strictly a marriage of affection. Our tastes, our feelings were congenial, and we were really a happy couple, with bright prospects in store." [58]

Around 1824 after the birth of their first child, Newel and Ann built a small frame home in Kirtland. In 1826 Newel purchased land across from his home and built a store that became known as the "white store" because of its color. He invited his friend Sidney to join him as a partner.

---

57   Elizabeth Ann Whitney, "A Leaf from an Autobiography," *Woman's Exponent*, August 15, 1878, 41.
58   Whitney, "Leaf from an Autobiography," August 15, 1878, 41.

The Whitney's Conversion

Religion was an important part of Ann and Newel Whitney's marriage, although they did not join any congregation. The study of the Bible was significantly important to them. Around 1828 they became acquainted with the Reformed Baptist (Campbellite) congregation of Sidney Rigdon in nearby Mentor, Ohio, and joined that movement.

Not long after the Ann and Newel united with Sidney's congregation, they had a remarkable spiritual experience:

Engraving of Newel K. Whitney.
Courtesy of the Joseph Smith Papers.

One night—it was midnight—as my husband and I, in our house at Kirtland, were praying to the father to be shown the way, the spirit rested upon us and a *cloud* overshadowed the house.

It was as though we were out of doors. The house passed away from our vision. We were not conscious of anything but the presence of the spirit and the cloud that was over us.

We were wrapped in the cloud. A solemn awe pervaded us. We saw the cloud and felt the spirit of the Lord.

Then we heard a voice out of the cloud, saying:

"Prepare to receive the word of the Lord, for it is coming."

At this we marveled greatly; but from that moment we knew that the word of the Lord was coming to Kirtland.[59]

They continued to worship with the Campbellites but understood that the Lord was soon to send them his word, and they looked forward with faith to its fulfillment. On October 29, 1830, four missionaries arrived in Kirtland, bringing with them the word of the Lord.

On hearing that missionaries had arrived in the area, Ann immediately wanted to listen to them preach. She recalled: "When I heard that these Elders

59   Edward W. Tullidge, *The Women of Mormondom* (New York, 1877), 41–42.

were preaching without money, or remuneration of any kind, . . . and that they were opposed to all priestcraft, I felt an earnest desire to hear their principles proclaimed, and to judge for myself."[60] As the missionaries shared their message, especially about the restoration of the primitive church and the authority of God to confer the Holy Ghost, Ann was convinced that these men were the fulfillment of the promise she and Newel had received that one night in their home. With excitement, she shared what she had learned from the missionaries with Newel and also announced her plans to be baptized. He asked her to wait until he had the opportunity to hear their message and find out for himself, but in her excitement for her newfound faith, she felt she could not wait. Ann was baptized in November 1830. Around this time, a handful of people gathered in the parlor of the Whitney home for a meeting that lasted all night as they sang and prophesied. Philo Dibble said of this meeting, "The heavens were opened and the Spirit of God filled the house and rested upon all the congregation to overflowing, little children not excepted."[61] At this meeting Newel became convinced of the truthfulness of the gospel and was baptized a few days later.

Joseph and Emma Smith Arrive in Kirtland

Interior of the Whitney Store. Newel K. Whitney was working here when the Prophet Joseph Smith walked in and introduced himself. Photo by Acacia E. Griffiths.

60   Whitney, "A Leaf from an Autobiography," *Woman's Exponent*, September 1, 1878, 51.

61   Philo Dibble, "Philo Dibble's Narrative," in *Early Scenes in Church History*, Faith-Promoting Series 8 (Salt Lake City: Juvenile Instructor Office, 1882; Salt Lake City: Bookcraft, 1968), 77.

In early February 1831, Newel Whitney was busy at work when a sleigh pulled in front of his store. A twenty-five-year-old man bounded in, came to the counter where Newel was working, reached his hand across the counter, and exclaimed: "Newell K Whitney, thou art the Man!" Surprised, Newel replied: "You have the advantage of me. I could not call you by name, as you have me." "I am Joseph the Prophet," the stranger declared. "You have prayed me here, now what do you want of me?"[62] Newel immediately took Joseph and Emma Smith across the street to his home to introduce them to his wife.

With Emma being 7 months pregnant and having just traveled nearly 230 miles in a sleigh in winter, the Whitneys invited Joseph and Emma to stay in their home. Ann Whitney recalled, "My husband brought them directly to our own house; we were more than glad to welcome them and share with them all the comforts and blessings we enjoyed."[63] Newel and Ann offered the Smiths a bedroom on the ground floor.

The Joseph and Emma shared the home with Newel, Ann, and their three children: Horace Kimball (age 7), Sarah Ann (age 6), and Orson Kimball (age 1). The Smiths stayed in this home for a few weeks until they moved to a house on the Morley Farm in March 1831. Joseph later wrote that while living with the Whitneys, he and Emma "received every kindness and attention which could be expected, and especially from Sister Whitney."[64] Ann later stated, "Joseph and Emma were very dear to me, and with my own hands I ministered to them, feeling it a privilege and an honor to do so."[65]

Mini-Devotional – "You Have Prayed Me Here"

Newel and Elizabeth Ann Whitney showed a sincere desire to seek after the truth. They prayed for the Lord to lead them to the true faith, and the Lord answered their prayers. Some answers came through miraculous visions and dreams. Other answers came through the people the Lord brought into their lives, like the missionaries who arrived in Kirtland, and the Prophet Joseph Smith, who said he came because of Newel's prayers. Take a moment to discuss or ponder the following:

---

62   Whitney, "Leaf from an Autobiography," September 1, 1878, 51.

63   Whitney, "Leaf from an Autobiography," September 1, 1878, 51.

64   Joseph Smith, *History of the Church of Jesus Christ of Latter-day Saints*, ed. B. H. Roberts (Salt Lake City, Deseret News, 1902), 1:146.

65   Elizabeth Ann Whitney, "Leaf from an Autobiography," August 15, 1878, 51.

- How has the Lord answered your prayers?
- How has the Lord answered your prayers through other people?

Edward Partridge: The First Bishop of the Church

Engraving of Edward Partridge.
Courtesy of Joseph Smith Papers.

In the revelation where the Lord commanded the Saints to gather to Ohio, he promised: "There I will give you my law" (Doctrine and Covenants 38:32). On February 4, 1831, the Lord began to fulfill that promise shortly after Joseph Smith arrived in Kirtland. In the Whitney home, the Lord revealed to Joseph: "Behold I give you a commandment, that ye shall assemble yourselves together to agree upon my word and by the prayer of your faith ye shall receive my law, that ye may know how to govern my church and have all things right before me" (Doctrine and Covenants 41:2–3). Joseph had struggled to help the Saints understand the proper way to administer the Church and build the Lord's kingdom, so the promise that the Lord would give them the law so they could "have all things right before him" must have brought great comfort to the Prophet. The Lord also revealed an additional step in building his kingdom by calling Edward Partridge to be the first bishop of the Church (verse 9).

Edward was born on August 27, 1793, in Pittsfield, Massachusetts, to William Partridge and Jemima Bidwell. In his youth, Edward learned the hatters trade and went into business near Albany, New York, with a partner and soon opened a shop in Painesville, Ohio. With the success of the shop in Ohio, Edward bought out his partner. In 1819, he married Lydia Clisbee, and they became the parents of seven children: Eliza Maria, Harriet Pamelia, Emily Dow, Caroline Ely, Lydia, a male child that died in infancy, and Edward Jr.[66]

---

66   Dean Jessee, "'Steadfastness and Patient Endurance': The Legacy of Edward
      Partridge," *Ensign*, June 1979.s

Early in his marriage, Edward found "'no beauty, comeliness or loveliness in the character of the God . . . preached by the sects'"[67] until he and his wife joined Sidney Rigdon's congregation in 1828. But even then, he believed that it was "absolutely necessary" for God to "again reveal himself to man and confer authority upon some one, or more, before his church could be built up in the last days, or any time after the apostasy."[68]

Shortly after the four missionaries who had been called to preach to the Lamanites arrived in Kirtland, Sidney visited Edward to share with him his newfound faith and encouraged him to listen to the missionaries. Even after the visit of the missionaries and a careful reading of the Book of Mormon, Edward remained cautious and stated that he could not be baptized until he had met the Prophet Joseph. Before long, Sidney and Edward departed to New York to meet Joseph and investigate his integrity. They traveled through "the Winter of Deep Snow"[69] and arrived at Smith family's previous home in Manchester, New York. They learned that Joseph was visiting his parents near Waterloo, so they continued their journey east. While listening to Joseph's message at a conference of Saints, Edward's heart was touched, and he was convinced of the truthfulness of the message of the restored gospel. After the conference, Edward asked the Prophet to baptize him that same day, but Joseph advised Edward to wait since he was probably exhausted from all his traveling. Through Joseph, the Lord also revealed his will to Edward and commanded him to preach the gospel (see Doctrine and Covenants 36). Two days later, on December 11, 1830, Joseph baptized Edward in the Seneca River,[70] and four days after that, Sidney ordained Edward an elder.[71]

Not two months later, the Lord "called [his] servant Edward Partridge . . . that he should be appointed by the voice of the church and ordained a bishop unto the church" (Doctrine and Covenants 41:9). Edward was also commanded "to leave his merchandise and to spend all his time in the labors of the church" (verse 9).

67   Andrew Jenson, "Partridge, Edward," *Latter-day Saint Biographical Encyclopedia: A Compilation of Biographical Sketches of Prominent Men and Women in the Church of Jesus Christ of Latter-day Saints* (Salt Lake City: Andrew Jenson History Company; The Deseret News, 1901), 1:218.

68   Milton V. Backman, Jr., *The Heavens Resound: A History of the Latter-Day Saints in Ohio 1830–1838* (Salt Lake City: Deseret Book Company, 1983), 16.

69   Mark L. Staker, *Hearken, O Ye People: The Historical Settings of Joseph Smith's Ohio Revelations,* (Salt Lake City: Greg Kofford Books, 2009), 75.

70   Backman, *Heavens Resound*, 40.

71   Hartt Wixom, *Edward Partridge: The First Bishop of The Church of Jesus Christ of Latter-day Saints* (Springville, UT: Cedar Fort, 1998), 144.

The Law of Consecration and Caring for the Poor: Doctrine and Covenants 42 and 44

A copy of the Book of Mormon in the parlor of the Whitney Home. The revelation containing the Law of Consecration was received here (Doctrine and Covenants 42).

On February 9, 1831, the Lord fulfilled his promise to reveal his law to the Saints in Ohio. This revelation is now found in section 42 of the Doctrine and Covenants and is commonly referred to as "the Law." In it, the Lord clarified spiritual laws and the calling of elders to preach and build the Lord's kingdom. The Lord also commanded the Saints to care for the poor and create an economic system to provide for all the members of the Church. He stated that in order to "remember" and care for the poor (verse 30), the Saints were to consecrate and lay their properties before the bishop and be made "stewards" over their own property (verse 32). The "residue" would be "consecrated unto the bishop . . . to administer to those who have not . . . that every man who has need may be amply supplied and receive according to his wants" (verse 33). Thus, the Lord expounded on the role of the bishop only days after calling Edward Partridge serve in the calling.

The Prophet received an additional revelation in the latter part of February declaring the need for the elders of the Church to gather for a conference (they designated June for the conference). The Lord also reminded the Saints of the importance of "the Law" they had received several days earlier. He command-ed them to "visit the poor and the needy and administer to their relief, that they may be kept until all things be done according to my law which ye have received" (Doctrine and Covenants 44:6). In June 1831, the Lord would again command the elders to "remember in all things the poor and the needy, the sick and the afflicted, for he that doeth not these things, the same is not [his] disciple" (Doctrine and Covenants 52:40). The role of bishop would develop over time and expand in responsibility, but from the beginning, the primary responsibility of the bishop was to care for the needs of all Saints, especially the poor and needy.

The Legacy of Edward Partridge

At the June 1831 conference, Edward Partridge was called to travel to Missouri, and while there, he was called to "plant" himself in Jackson County. He felt the pain of leaving everything he knew in Ohio and the challenge that a move to the frontier would mean for his family. He wrote to his wife, Lydia, explaining the difficulties of the area and left the decision up to her as to whether she and the children would join him in Missouri. Undaunted by the challenge, Lydia and the Partridge children left for Missouri later that year. In their travels and years in Missouri, they would experience extreme trials.[72] In 1833 amongst the mob violence, Edward was tarred and feathered, and he and his family were forced to flee from county to county. During these diffi-cult times in Missouri, he continued to serve as bishop and even served mul-tiple missions in harsh conditions, facing much loneliness. In 1838, he was imprisoned in the Richmond Jail and later recorded: "We were confined in a large open room where the cold northern blast penetrated freely; our fires were small, and our allowance for wood and for food scanty. They gave us not even a blanket to lie upon. . . . The vilest of the vile did guard us and treat us like dogs; yet we bore our oppressions without murmuring."[73] He was then forced to flee the state without his family. After enduring many trials, he was reunit-ed with his family in Illinois, and together they made their way to Commerce (later Nauvoo) where they "pitched a tent under a large elm tree" for about a year.[74]

---

72   Jessee, "'Steadfastness and Patient Endurance.'"
73   Jessee, "'Steadfastness and Patient Endurance.'"
74   Jessee, "'Steadfastness and Patient Endurance.'"

Edward was appointed as the bishop of Nauvoo's Upper Ward and served continuously even though he became extremely sick and suffered from chills and fever. His daughter Emily Dow Partridge Young recalled, "He did not feel as though he could spend time to be sick,"[75] and succumbed to his sickness and died on May 27, 1840 at the age of 46. Edward had literally given his wealth and his health to the Lord. Reflecting on her father's service, Emily wrote:

> When I look and remember the great responsibility resting upon my father as bishop—his poverty and privations and hardships he had to endure, the accusations of false brethren, the grumbling of the poor, and the persecution of our enemies, I do not wonder at his early death; and when I remember his conversations with my mother, and can now comprehend in my mature years, his extreme weariness of soul, it brings to my mind a clause of his blessing, which says, "Thou shalt stand in thy office until thou shalt desire to resign it that thou mayest rest for a little season."[76]

Joseph Smith said of him, "[Edward] was a pattern of piety, and one of the Lord's great men, known by his steadfastness, and patient endurance to the end."[77] His family continued to build his legacy and the Church he loved. Most of them traveled with the Saints to the Salt Lake Valley.

---

75   Emily Dow Partridge Young, "Incidents of the Life of a Mormon Girl," n.d., 174, MS 5220, Church History Library, Salt Lake City.

76   Young, "Incidents," 80–81.

77   "History of Joseph Smith," *Times and Seasons* 4, no. 21 (September 15, 1843): 320, https://contentdm.lib.byu.edu/digital/collection/NCMP1820-1846/id/8578.

Mrs. Hubble and False Claims of Authority:
Doctrine and Covenants 43

Detail of a fruit tree growing near the Whitney Home. Photo by Acacia E. Griffiths.

Shortly after the Lord revealed "the Law" in February 1831, a challenge arose among the Saints. The early Saints were influenced by a belief in a universal priesthood and the fact that all members were entitled to revelation. A new convert was believed to possess significant spiritual gifts, causing "some members of the Church" to be "disturbed by people making false claims as revelators" (Doctrine and Covenants 43, section heading). Her name was probably Laura Fuller Hubbell, but throughout Church history, she is commonly known as "Mrs. Hubble."[78]

In describing Mrs. Hubble's influence when she came to Kirtland, Joseph Smith said she was "a woman . . . with great pretentions to revealing commandments, laws and other curious matters."[79] John Whitmer recorded that she "professed to be a prophetess of the Lord and professed to have many

---

78   There is some question as to the actual name of this convert. There was a Laura
      Fuller Hubbell who was the older sister of an early convert, Edson Fuller.
      However, Hayden, in his *Early Disciples of the Western Reserve*, lists a Mrs. Louisa
      Hubbell, who was a member of the Disciples of Christ, temporarily accepted the
      restored gospel, then rejoined the Disciples shortly thereafter.
79   Joseph Smith History, vol. A-1, 101, JSP.

revelations," and because she appeared "sanctimonious," some Saints "were not able to detect her in her hypocracy."[80] Ezra Booth added that she "so ingratiated herself into the esteem and favor of some of the Elders, that they received her, as a person commissioned to act a conspicuous part of Mormonizing the world."[81] Her revelatory claims bore witness of the Book of Mormon but also indicated "that she should become a teacher in the Church of Christ."[82] The issue that challenged the Saints was whether individual members could be directed by their own divine revelation to be ordained teachers and receive authority to direct Church administration.

Finding it "necessary to inquire of the Lord,"[83] the Prophet received a revelation so the Saints would "not be deceived" (Doctrine and Covenants 43:6). The Lord said, "Ye have received a commandment for a law unto my church, through him whom I have appointed unto you to receive commandments and revelations from my hand" (Doctrine and Covenants 43:2), and "there is none other appointed unto you to receive commandments and revelations until he be taken" (verse 3). This revelation could be considered part of "the Law" because it was revealed in between the two "official" days when all of "the Law" was revealed and because the Lord himself said "this shall be a law unto you" (verse 5). The Saints were not to "receive . . . the teachings of any that shall come before [them] as revelations or commandments" (verse 5) in order that they "may not be deceived, that [they] may know they are not of [God]" (verse 6). He then made the fulfillment of the Saints' desires for the "glories" and the "mysteries of the kingdom" contingent on upholding Joseph "by the prayer of faith" and by providing "for him food and raiment, and whatsoever thing he needeth" (verses 12–13).

The Lord reiterated his design for Church leadership to address the Hubble problem. He repeated what he had already stated in "the Law": "He that is ordained of me shall come in at the gate and be ordained as I have told you before, to teach those revelations which you have received and shall receive through him whom I have appointed" (verse 7). This revelation helped the Saints better understand Joseph Smith's role in receiving revelation and authority to lead the Church. However, throughout the year 1831, Lord gave many other revelations dealing with the matter of false spirits and leaders and

---

80   Joseph Smith History, vol. A-1, 101, JSP; John Whitmer, History, 1831–circa 1847, 18, JSP.

81   Ezra Booth, "Letter VIII," *Mormonism Unvailed*, ed. E. D. Howe (Painesville, OH, 1834), 216.

82   John Whitmer, History, 1831–circa 1847, 18, JSP.

83   Joseph Smith History, vol. A-1, 101, JSP.

the need for personal revelation. Soon after Joseph received this revelation now found in Doctrine and Covenants 43, the situation with Mrs. Hubble quieted down, and she "returned to the place from when she came."[84]

Priesthood Healing of Elsa Johnson's Arm

Elsa and John Johnson came to Kirtland after having a powerful experience studying the Book of Mormon. The couple decided to travel to Kirtland to meet the Prophet Joseph Smith. During a small gathering of people in the Whitney home parlor, the topic of spiritual gifts was brought up, prompting Elsa to ask the Prophet whether the power to heal had been restored. She had been afflicted for two years with "chronic rheumatism in the shoulder," [85] and her right arm had been virtually useless. He replied that healing had been restored, but he waited until the next day for the ideal time to lay his hands upon her and pronounce a healing blessing by the authority of the priesthood. Elsa's right arm was instantly restored, as strong and useful as her left.[86]

The healing of Elsa's arm in March 1831, possibly the first recorded priesthood healing in this dispensation, occurred in the same place where a month earlier the Lord had revealed his will concerning the restoration of this spiritual gift. "And the elders of the church, two or more, shall be called, and shall pray for and lay their hands upon [the sick] in my name" (Doctrine and Covenants 42:44).

Bishop Newel K. Whitney: Doctrine and Covenants 72

The revelation now found in section 72 of the Doctrine and Covenants was given to Joseph Smith while he was in Kirtland. While the exact location is unknown, it is possible that it was received at the Whitney home. By December 1831, Edward Partridge had relocated to Missouri, and Newel K.

---

84   Booth, "Letter VIII," 216.

85   Luke Johnson, "History of Luke Johnson," *The Latter-day Saints' Millennial Star* 26, no. 53 (December 31, 1864): 834, https://contentdm.lib.byu.edu/digital/collection/MStar/id/27915.

86   Philo Dibble, "Philo Dibble's Narrative," *Early Scenes in Church History*, Faith-Promoting Series 8 (Salt Lake City: Juvenile Instructor Office, 1882; Salt Lake City: Bookcraft, 1968), 79.

Whitney was acting as "agent" to the bishop in Kirtland. On December 4, the Lord revealed: "It is expedient in me for a bishop to be appointed unto" (Doctrine and Covenants 72:2). "My servant Newel K. Whitney is the man who shall be appointed and ordained unto this power" (verse 8). Upon learning of his call to serve, Newel stated: "I cannot see a Bishop in myself, Brother Joseph; but if you say it's the Lord's will, I'll try." "You need not take my word alone" Joseph said. "Go and ask Father for yourself." Newel went to his bedroom to pray and "heard a voice from heaven: 'The strength is in me.'" Newel then went to Joseph and accepted the office.[87] Ann Whitney stated that her husband "felt that it would require a vast amount of patience, of perseverance and of wisdom to magnify his calling."[88]

Newel served faithfully as bishop in Kirtland for many years and also as a member of the United Firm. His long hours of devotion caused him to be away from home, but Ann said of their sacrifice: "During all these absences and separations from my husband, I never felt to murmur, or complain in the least . . . yet I was more than satisfied to have him give all, time, talents, and ability into the service of the Kingdom of God; and the changes in our circumstances and associations which were consequent upon our embracing the Gospel, never caused me a moment's sorrow."[89]

---

87   B. H. Roberts, *A Comprehensive History of the Church* (Salt Lake City: Deseret Book Company, 1930), 1:271; Staker, *Hearken O Ye People*, 126.

88   Elizabeth Ann Whitney, "Leaf from an Autobiography," August 15, 1878, 71.

89   Elizabeth Ann Whitney, "Leaf from an Autobiography," August 15, 1878, 71.

The Feast of the Poor

The entrance to the Newel K. and Elizabeth Ann Whitney home. Photo by Acacia E. Griffiths.

In September 1832, Joseph Smith received another a revelation concerning Newel K. Whitney: "[He] also should travel round about and among all the churches, searching after the poor to administer to their wants" (Doctrine and Covenants 84:112). In January 1836, Ann and Newel hosted a three-day feast for all the poor, ill, and needy in the area. Of this event, Joseph stated: "Attended a sumptuous feast at Bishop Newel K. Whitney's. This feast was after the order of the Son of God, the lame, the halt, and the blind were invited, according to the instructions of the Savior."[90] Ann and Newel continually sought to search for the poor and to administer to their wants.

The Legacy of Newel K. and Elizabeth Ann Whitney

The Whitney family continued to serve and faithfully follow the Prophet and the Saints. They left Kirtland in the fall of 1838 and traveled to Missouri, where they were soon forced to flee to Illinois. In Illinois, Newel K. Whitney

---

90   Joseph Smith History, Journal, January 7, 1836, JSP.

served as bishop of the Middle Ward in Commerce (Nauvoo). In 1842, Ann Whitney was called to be a counselor to Emma Smith in the first Relief Society presidency in Nauvoo. In 1844, Newel was called as "first bishop" of the church. While in Nauvoo, the Whitneys accepted and entered plural marriage. Newel would later be married to seven additional women. The Whitneys migrated to Utah in 1848, and Newel served as bishop of the Salt Lake City Eighteenth Ward. He died September 23, 1850, at the age of fifty-five. Ann continued in her service in the Church and was revered by the Saints as "Mother Whitney." She served as the second counselor to Eliza R Snow in the Relief Society from 1880 until her death at age eighty-one on February 15, 1882. The Witneys not only provided a home for Joseph and Emma Smith when they needed it, but they left a legacy of faith for all members of the Church.

Mini-Devotional – "A Feast for the Poor"

Newel and Elizabeth Ann Whitney became two of the most influential members of the Church because of their generosity and kindness to those around them. The volunteered their resources and their time to assist other less fortunate members of the Church and left behind a legacy of service that still influences the Church today. Newel and Edward Partridge's service as the first bishops in the Church set the standard for all Church leaders to follow today in being mindful of the people in their stewardships, especially the poor. Elizabeth Ann's sacrifices to help those around her served as a forerunner to the work of the righteous sisters throughout the Church. Take a moment to ponder their legacy and then discuss or reflect on the following:

- How does serving others help us to draw closer to the Savior and Heavenly Father?
- What are some small (or large) acts of service that you can do for the people around you?

Significant events at these locations:

- In 1819 members constructed a schoolhouse that was used not only for children's education but also for Church meetings and ordinances.

- In 1824 Newel K. Whitney established an ashery that provided income for the Church.

- In 1827 Peter French built a tavern that functioned as an inn, store, meeting place, and eventually a Church printing press.

- In 1832 Sidney Rigdon gained possession of the Mason Tannery, and Newel K. and Elizabeth Ann Whitney consecrated their property.

- In 1883 the Church purchased the Peter French Farm, including the tavern, and Joel Hills Johnson helped design and construct a sawmill on the property to assist in building the Kirtland Temple.

Historic Kirtland: Other Special Buildings

In January 1830, Joseph Smith received a commandment to "go to the Ohio; and there I will give unto you my law; and there you shall be endowed with power from on high" (Doctrine and Covenants 38:32). Over the eight years that followed, Kirtland, Ohio, became the home of Joseph and Emma Smith's family and a center of Church activity. The buildings at Historic Kirtland are where some of the most important revelations were given to Joseph. Additionally, the Saints who lived and worked at these historic structures became some of the earliest leaders of the Church, who helped build a strong foundation for the Church so it could expand.

Visitors who walk among these buildings at Historic Kirtland will be able to envision the daily life and appreciate the sacrifices of these early Saints. Here, the Saints worked hard to live the law of consecration and establish a home where other early converts could gather and worship in harmony. During this time, Newel K. and Elizabeth Ann Whitney served as key leaders of the community. Newel was called as the presiding bishop in Kirtland in 1831 (see Doctrine and Covenants 72:7–8). Their store in Kirtland became a hub for Church activity. So many significant events took place at this site that it is covered in a separate chapter. Many of the businesses in Kirtland were owned by the Whitneys and operated by the Kirtland Saints. This business model constructed an economic engine that allowed the Saints to provide for themselves and the converts who gathered to the area. Some of the buildings of historical significance at Historic Kirtland include the tannery, inn, livery, sawmill, ashery, and schoolhouse.

Tannery

A home now stands on the site of the Kirtland tannery, found next to the Whitney Store.
Photo by Casey Paul Griffiths.

Just east of the Whitney Store stands the building that housed a tannery, but it now houses the Kirtland Historic Sites mission president and companion. In 1832, Arnold Mason, who was not a Latter-day Saint, constructed the original building adjacent to Stoney Brook since the tannery required a ready water supply in order to operate. As the name suggests, the business of a tannery was to process animal hide into leather. The resident tanner would store the hides in the building and perform most of the tanning labor outside in the tanyard, where large vats could be continually filled with water from Stoney Brook.

The process for producing high-quality leather was time-consuming, labor-intensive, and odorous. It could require as long as a year to produce the highest quality leathers. Tanners had to crush and grind oak or hemlock bark until it became a powdery substance called *tannin*. Then they would add the tannin to water vats to produce an extremely harsh soaking solution. Skins were soaked in the tannin solution, scoured, cured, and rinsed multiple times.

The Mason Tannery in Kirtland sold the leather it produced to several crafts-men in the area who made clothing, shoes, saddles, or harnesses.

In a high priest meeting on April 2, 1833, Ezra Thayer was directed to offer to buy the Mason Tannery. The United Firm was supposed to manage the transaction, but the organization was dissolved before the purchase was finished. Nevertheless, the transaction was completed more than a year later, and the tannery and several other properties were distributed to Church members who had been in the United Firm. The Lord directed that Sidney Rigdon receive the tannery as well as the lot and home in which he and his family were living, which was near the temple site (Doctrine and Covenants 104:20). Sidney's recent ordination as first counselor in the First Presidency precluded him from devoting much time to running a tanning business, so others were left to the task. He eventually sold the tannery to his mother, Nancy Rigdon, in October 1836.

Johnson Inn and Whitney & Gilbert Livery Stable

This small home now stands on the site of the Gilbert Livery Stable. Photo by Acacia E. Griffiths.

As with most taverns or inns of the time, the building now called the Johnson Inn was originally built as a two-story home. Peter French, a well-known community leader, constructed the home on his 103-acre farm, which included flat land and a slope up to a plateau. Located at the busy intersection shared by the Whitney Store, the building functioned as the Peter French Tavern as well as a store by 1827. As Saints continued to gather to Kirtland, Church leaders realized there wasn't enough land for them to settle on, so in April 1833, the Church purchased the French farm, including the tavern, for $5,000. With the tavern on the northern end of the property, Church leaders designated the southern end, which was on the plateau, for temple construction and lots for homes. The Lord directed that "Newel K. Whitney take charge" as agent for the property (Doctrine and Covenants 96:2), and Thomas Knight operated the store through the summer. John Johnson gained control of the tavern in the fall, moved his family into it, operated it as an inn, and then received stewardship over it when the United Firm was dissolved. He bought it from the Church in 1836 for $5,000, the original selling price of the entire French property, then arranged for his son John Johnson Jr. to take ownership six months later.

The rebuilt John Johnson Inn at Historic Kirtland. Photo by Casey Paul Griffiths.

The John Johnson Inn at Historic Kirtland. Photo by Acacia E. Griffiths.

Like most inns of the day, the inn provided rooms and meals for passengers on stagecoach lines as well as for independent travelers. It also supported community life by providing a place for socializing and entertainment in its second-floor ballroom. After the Church purchased the French Farm, the United Firm used the building as meeting place, museum, social hall, printing shop, and office building, but it also still served as an inn. In August 1833, after the Missouri printing office had been destroyed by a mob, the Lord directed that "the work of the printing" be accomplished in Kirtland (Doctrine and Covenants 94:12). Oliver Cowdery and Frederick G. Williams set up a temporary printing office in the inn in December after a press had been acquired. During the meeting to dedicate the Kirtland printing office on December 18, 1833, the Prophet introduced the office of evangelist, or patriarch, to the Church and gave the first patriarchal blessings in this dispensation to Oliver Cowdery, Joseph Smith Sr., Lucy Mack Smith, and Hyrum, Samuel, and William Smith. Joseph Smith Sr. was ordained as Patriarch to the Church the following year, and he actively bestowed blessings until his death six years later in Nauvoo, Illinois. Three months after their calling as Apostles, the Quorum of the Twelve met at the Johnson Inn to begin their first mission together at 2:00 a.m. on May 4, 1835. They met so early in the morning because they were planning to board a steamboat twelve miles away at Fairport Harbor on

Lake Erie.[91] The inn was also one of the places where the Egyptian papyri and mummies that Joseph Smith Jr. had purchased were on display.

Across the road just east of the Johnson Inn is the Kirtland Heritage Center, a small home-like building that traditionally has kept historical records so that visitors can look up their Kirtland ancestors. However, this function is now performed in the Johnson Inn. The center sits on the site of the Whitney & Gilbert Livery Stable, which served as an important companion to the services provided by the inn. Whether traveling individually, or on a stage line, the livery stable provided a stable and food for travelers' horses.

Sawmill

The sawmill at Historic Kirtland. Photo by Casey Paul Griffiths.

---

91   Record of the Twelve, April 26, 1835 and Record of the Twelve, May 4–9, 1835, JSP.

A closer view of the sawmill at Historic Kirtland. Photo by Casey Paul Griffiths..

Sawmills were an important element of a strong economic base for a small community. They provided the lumber for skilled craftsmen like carpenters, coopers, wheelwrights, and cabinetmakers, and these craftsmen, in turn, dramatically improved the quality of home construction and life in general. Peter French built the first sawmill in Kirtland, and its prominence, along with his gristmill for grinding grain, caused people to refer to the Kirtland area as Kirtland Mills. Azariah Lyman and his brother-in-law Austin Loud purchased Peter's original sawmill and gristmill shortly after the Saints began gathering to Kirtland.

After receiving the command to build a temple, Church leaders purchased a sixteen-acre wood lot for $550 in March 1833 just upstream from the Lyman and Loud sawmill, suggesting they probably intended to hire Lyman and Loud to provide lumber for the temple's construction. Although they may have provided some lumber for early construction, Lyman and Loud already had large contracts to build churches in nearby communities. The arrival of Joel Hills Johnson, a convert who was also a millwright, spawned the decision for the Church to construct its own sawmill. Ironically, this decision created competition for Lyman and Loud, and they became angry with the Church. They went so far as to organize a campaign to try to drive the Saints from Kirtland by refusing to sell them grain. Their efforts failed, which led them to eventually leave the milling business.

Demonstration in the Kirtland sawmill of how the pulpits in the Kirtland temple were crafted. Photo by Casey Paul Griffiths.

Joel Hills Johnson's first assignment relating to temple construction was brickmaking. However, Joel's bricks crumbled when fired, so the Saints decided to build the temple out of stone and a nearby quarry was located. But the temple still needed wood. Starting in November 1833, Joel worked with other local men for six months to build a sawmill he had designed. They built the mill on Stoney Brook on a portion of the recently purchased French property so the waterwheel could generate power for the saw and other machinery. Unlike other sawmills, this sawmill was constructed primarily to provide lumber for interior woodwork. Craftsmen operated lathes and other machinery in the mill to produce intricate woodwork. All of the lumber used for the finish work in the temple was processed at Joel's sawmill. It also supplied lumber for homes and other Church buildings, such as the printing office at the northwest corner of the temple. Thus, the mill provided work for newly gathered Church members, and later it was used to produce funds to help the Church meet temple construction debts.

The process of preparing lumber for the temple began with experienced lumbermen who selected which trees to use. Local farmers with experience in felling trees on their own lands were hired to cut down these designated trees using handheld axes. They would make a large cut—the undercut—on the side of the tree that aligned with the direction they wanted the tree to fall. The smaller, back cut was made on the opposite side, which weakened the tree and caused it to fall. Its branches were removed, and they were stacked and then pushed into the stream, where they floated to a location near the sawmill. They were then restacked and dragged to the mill. Using logways—diagonally laid timbers that created a type of ramp—sawmill workers rolled the logs into the mill and then slid other ramps into place to roll one log at a time onto the saw carriage.

The Stoney Brook water that powered the mill led into a dam south of the mill. To operate the mill, a gate was lowered above the wheel, allowing the water to flow into the buckets of which the wheel was comprised. The relatively low amount of fall as well as water quantity dictated that the waterwheel was a breast wheel, which means that water flowed into the middle of the wheel. A large gear was attached to the wheel, which, in turn, powered a small gear connected to a shaft in the mill basement. This small gear powered the up and down movement of the sash saw at a rate around one hundred strokes per minute. The carriage that pushed the log through the moving saw blade was also powered by a metal bar that was attached to the saw sash.

A woodworking shop was constructed to the side of the saw, and the waterwheel also supplied power for a lathe and a power molding plane via a leather belt that connected to an overhead shaft. The temple's beautiful priesthood pulpits, ornate moldings, doors on the pulpits, and interior window sashes were all constructed in this shop. Lumber from the sawmill was also used to construct the roof, the gables, and the tower. Woodwork specifications came from four sources: the verbal descriptions provided by the First Presidency's vision of the temple, planning that occurred during the temple's exterior construction, the workers' own building experience, and contemporary carpenters' manuals in popular use, including *Asher Benjamin's American Builder's Companion*.

Because newly cut lumber warps and cracks if used for construction purposes, it has to be seasoned, or dried out. Two valid methods of seasoning wood are open-air drying and kiln drying, which uses a special drying furnace to accelerate the process. The cut wood from the Church's sawmill was kiln dried; however, kiln drying in those days was not without risks, and the kiln near the sawmill caught fire several times. The exact location of the kiln the workers used is not known, only that it was near the mill.

The sawmill provided a needed community service, but more importantly, it provided opportunities for consecrated offerings of resources, time, and labor. Most of the labor to run the sawmill was donated, and the land upon which it stood was one of several consecrations provided by Newel K. and Elizabeth Ann Whitney. The sawmill that visitors see today is a reproduction of the original.

Ashery

The rebuilt Kirtland Ashery. Photo by Casey Paul Griffiths.

Merchants in the 1820s and 1830s often added asheries to their business enterprises. Using the bartering system, customers could pay for store commodities with ashes from their fireplaces or from trees they felled while preparing cropland. With a minimal investment, merchants could then turn a rather substantial profit by chemically transforming these ashes into potash or pearl ash. Pearl ash was often used to create soap and glass. Potash was an important ingredient in manufacturing alum, saltpeter, soap, glass, tanned leather, gunpowder, paper, bleached cotton textiles, and processed woolen goods. Today, its principal use is fertilizer.

Interior of the Kirtland Ashery. Missionaries at the site offer demonstrations for how the ashery was used to create potash, pearlash, and other products. Photo by Casey Paul Griffiths.

Newel K. Whitney first established a small ashery in 1824 on a site near Stoney Brook, having purchased property from Peter French for that purpose two years earlier for $26, along with water rights to a spring on the hill south of his property for another $10. Although the brook could have provided water for operating the ashery, clear spring water was much preferred. He replaced his first ashery with a larger one in 1828, then in 1832, he consecrated this prosperous enterprise to the Church. Newel's partner, Sidney Gilbert, probably provided the day-to-day management of the ashery until he moved to Missouri in 1831. It provided cash income for the Church and was an essential part of Kirtland's economy. The 1828 structure was a rough-timber frame building with vertical exterior siding and a shingle roof; it measured sixty feet long and about twenty feet wide. A small adjoining office located on the west side measured twelve feet by ten feet. Shuttered window openings on the north and south sides and on the east end were used to regulate ventilation and light.

Newel K. Whitney's ashery required four or five adult workers along with additional teenage assistants in order to operate. Orson Hyde worked in Newel's store, but sometimes he also worked in the ashery. The ashery workers wore leather aprons and long leather gloves to protect their skin from the hot and caustic chemicals used in the ashery process. Workers also wore long-sleeved clothing for protection while packing the finished products, so working in an ashery was a hot, uncomfortable, and somewhat dangerous occupation.

Ashes were shoveled into rectangular wooden frames known as hoppers, which were open at the top and narrowed toward another opening in the bottom. The ashes sat near the bottom opening on a six-inch filter made of twigs and straw. After the ashes were tamped down, holes were poked in the tops of the ashes. Spring water traveled by wooden pipes to a cistern below the ashery and then was pumped into a large wooden reservoir above the hoppers. Water ran out of the wooden reservoir through spigots and troughs to the fill the hoppers. As the water dripped through the ashes over a two- or three-day period, it extracted alkali, creating an amber-colored liquid known as lye, which was collected in wooden buckets below the hoppers. The lye was tested in the small office on the end of the ashery to determine its alkalinity. If the alkalinity was insufficient, the entire bucket was sent back through the ashes a second time and sometimes a third. If the alkalinity was sufficient, then it was poured into a large wooden cask to await further chemical processing.

Lye from the cask was carried by buckets to one of four large, cast-iron kettles that sat on the furnace. The kettles were forty inches in diameter and two feet deep, and they weighed more than six hundred pounds. The lye was boiled and stirred frequently for approximately twelve hours until it boiled down to a thick syrup known as black salts. As the syrup cooled, it became a solid mass of potash, which was then turned out of the kettle and broken up with an axe. If a purer chemical composition was required, the chunks were further heated in an arched, reverberatory oven to a temperature of nearly one thousand degrees until all volatile carbon was burned off, thus producing a chunk of white pearl ash. The Erie and Ohio-Erie Canals provided ready access to markets in the south and east as well as across the Atlantic Ocean to Great Britain. One barrel could sell for between $100 and $200.

As mentioned previously, Newel K. and Elizabeth Ann Whitney consecrated their ashery, store, and other businesses to the Church. Their contributions were vital for the economic well-being of the Church and for the Lord's command to care for the poor. As the United Firm was created in 1833 to act as a business management entity, the ashery became one of the businesses operated in trust and proved to be the core of the Church's financial resources. When the United Firm was dissolved by the Lord in 1834, he directed that its assets be divided among its members as stewardships. Newel was appointed the ashery, among other assets, which he operated until 1835 or 1836 when it burned down.

The reconstruction of the Kirtland ashery provided new insights into how the Word of Wisdom (Doctrine and Covenants 89) was received by the local Saints. In 2000, during an archaeological dig just south of the site of the ashery, historian Mark Staker found several pipe fragments. It is possible these fragments are remnants of the pipes thrown into the fireplace of the Whitney Store when the Word of Wisdom was first revealed. Mark and his team dated a layer above the pipe fragments to 1842. The fragments themselves are in a location that might align them with the time when the Word of Wisdom was given, though it is difficult assign a precise date.

Pipe fragments discovered during the archaeological excavations of the Kirtland Ashery.
Photo courtesy of Church History Museum.

Given these factors, there is a good chance that some, if not all, of the pipe fragments came from the Whitney fireplace. The name *Johnson* is stamped on the side of one of the pipe stems, which may indicate that the pipe belonged to Lyman Johnson, who was present at the time the Word of Wisdom was revealed. Zebedee Coltrin, who was also present, recalled: "When the Word of Wisdom was first presented by the Prophet Joseph (as he came out of the translating room) and was read to the School, there were twenty out of the twenty-one who used tobacco, and they all immediately threw their tobacco and pipes into the fire. There were members as follows: Joseph Smith, Hyrum Smith, William Smith, Fredrick G. Williams, Orson Hyde (who had the charge of the school), Zebedee Coltrin, Sylvester Smith, Joseph Smith Sen., Levi Hancock, Martin Harris, Sidney Rigdon, Newell K. Whitney, Samuel

H. Smith, John Murdock, Lyman Johnson, and Ezra Thayer."[92] The pipe fragments found in the Kirtland ashery might be linked to Lyman Johnson, though absolute certainty is impossible because there were many Johnsons in the area, or the name may be from the manufacturer.[93] However, the pipe fragments are further evidence of a story we are still living: the current prophets and apostles leading the Church continue to receive guidance from God on how we can best manage the sacred stewardship of the human body.

Kirtland Flats Schoolhouse

The Kirtland Flats Schoolhouse. Photo by Casey Paul Griffiths.

The site of the Kirtland Flats Schoolhouse was first occupied in 1814 by a small log school structure, which was replaced by a larger, frame schoolhouse in 1819. The schoolhouse operated as an informal, grassroots endeavor until it became a district school in 1828. The subjects covered in early schools were spelling, reading, penmanship, arithmetic, and sometimes geography.

---

92   School of the Prophets Salt Lake City meeting minutes, October 3, 1883, CR 390
      5, Church History Library, Salt Lake City.

93   Mark L. Staker, "'Thou Art the Man:' Newel K. Whitney in Ohio," *BYU Studies*
      42, no. 1 (2003): 107.

The first converts of the Kirtland area met in homes for worship. However, as the Church continued to grow, a large congregation met in the schoolhouse, and smaller groups met in homes. The schoolhouse continued to be used for worship, even after the temple was completed. Worship meetings included Sunday morning preaching meetings, Sunday afternoon sacrament services, and Sunday and Tuesday evening prayer meetings.

The Sunday morning prayer meetings usually began at 10 a.m. with prayer and congregational hymn singing. One or two priesthood holders were called on to speak, often including Joseph Smith Jr., Sidney Rigdon, Oliver Cowdery, or one of the other early Church leaders. Speakers often expounded upon Church doctrine using a selected scriptural passage as a text. The meetings then concluded with more hymn singing and prayer. However, before the meeting adjourned, those desiring to be baptized were invited to stand, and during the intermission that preceded the sacrament meetings, these people would often be baptized in the Chagrin River just north of the schoolhouse.

The afternoon sacrament meetings also began with prayer, hymn singing, and one or two talks. Priesthood leaders conducted Church business and performed ordinances, including the confirmation of recent converts, priesthood ordinations, and baby blessings. Priesthood holders blessed and passed the sacrament to the congregation at the end of the meeting using wine "made new among you" (Doctrine and Covenants 27:4), and someone would deliver a talk during the sacrament administration.

Evening prayer meetings began at dusk. They were less formal but did include preaching, and both men and women participated in praying, singing hymns, bearing testimony, and speaking in tongues. Joseph Smith Jr. recorded that one evening he "attended prayer-meeting, opened it, and exhorted the brethren and sisters about one hour. The Lord poured out his Spirit and some glorious things were spoken in the gift of tongues and interpreted, concerning the redemption of Zion."[94]

Daniel Tyler once described attending the schoolhouse for a prayer meeting in which Joseph Smith Jr. offered prayer. As the meeting began, Daniel observed that the Prophet appeared sorrowful, and tears poured down his cheeks. He assumed that Joseph's sadness was because of the actions of his brother William. Following the opening hymn, Joseph stood to pray, but rather than facing the congregation, he bowed on his knees and faced the wall. Daniel then related the following:

---

94   Joseph Smith History, B-1, 630, The Joseph Smith Papers, JSP.

I had heard men and women pray—especially the former—from the most ignorant . . . to the most learned and eloquent, but never until then had I heard a man address his Maker as though He was present listening as a kind father would listen to the sorrows of a dutiful child. Joseph was at that time unlearned, but that prayer, which was to a considerable extent in behalf of those who accused him of having gone astray and fallen into sin, that the Lord would forgive them and open their eyes that they might see aright—that prayer, I say, to my humble mind, partook of the learning and eloquence of heaven. There was no ostentation, no raising of the voice as by enthusiasm, but a plain conversational tone, as a man would address a present friend. It appeared to me as though, in case the vail were taken away, I could see the Lord standing facing His humblest of all servants. . . . It was the crowning, so to speak, of all the prayers I ever heard.[95]

Mini-Devotional—The Law of Consecration

Elizabeth Ann and Newel K. Whitney demonstrated their absolute commitment to God and his Church by their willingness to consecrate their rather substantial worldly possessions. Today we are also commanded to consecrate all that we are and have to building up the Church. Discuss examples of people from your family history or from other sources who demonstrated the spirit of consecration as the Whitneys did. Contemplate how willing you are to give your all in the service of God, whether it be your time, your talents, your possessions, or even yourself.

- Like the Whitneys, what are some ways that your family, including your ancestors, have consecrated to build up the kingdom of God?
- What talents and gifts do you have that can be consecrated to the Lord?

---

95   Daniel Tyler, "Recollections of the Prophet Joseph Smith," *Juvenile Instructor* (February 1892), 127–28.

Significant events at this location:

- Joseph, Emma, Julia, and Joseph Smith III moved from the Whitney Store apartment to their own home, sometime between November 1833 and February 1834.

- The Lord gave counsel to Joseph Smith concerning the persecutions in Missouri and instructed him to call Zion's Camp at this location.

- Joseph was living in this home when the Egyptian mummies and papyri fragments associated with the Book of Abraham were purchased in July 1835.

- Early parts of the Book of Abraham translation took place at the Smith home from the fall of 1833 until early 1836.

- Doctrine and Covenants 101, 102, 103, 104, 106, and parts of 107 were received at the Smiths' Kirtland home.

THE JOSEPH AND EMMA SMITH HOME

*The Joseph and Emma Home shortly before it was restored
to its original appearance. Photo by Acacia E. Griffiths.*

The home of Joseph and Emma Smith, located just north of the Kirtland Temple and the nearby cemetery, was acquired from the Community of Christ by The Church of Jesus Christ of Latter-day Saints in 2012, along with other sacred historical sites. After several years of historical assessment and careful planning, the Church restored the Smith home and Joseph's store in the summer of 2022. The store is located directly across the street from the Smith home. Touring these buildings offers some rare insights into the life of Joseph and Emma's family during their time in Kirtland. It represents an important location in the collection of places the Prophet and his family lived, and thus, it is a place made sacred by revelations and other events central to the Restoration. It was the first home Joseph and Emma actually owned in Ohio. Their second child to live to adulthood, Frederick Granger Williams Smith, was also born there on June 20, 1836. The child was named for Joseph's second counselor and good friend Frederick G. Williams. The Smith family lived in this home until January 1838 when Joseph was directed by revelation to flee Kirtland in order to escape the murderous threats of former members and angry mobs.

Doctrine and Covenants 101: The Saints' Removal from Zion

It has long been believed that the Prophet moved into this home in February 1834, but recent evidence suggests that the move may have occurred as early as November 1833. It may not be possible to determine the precise date. Depending on when Joseph's family moved into the home, it is possible that this is location where he received the revelation now found in Doctrine and Covenants 101. In this revelation, the Lord explained why he allowed the Saints to be driven from Zion in Jackson County in November 1833:

> I, the Lord, have suffered the affliction to come upon them, wherewith they have been afflicted, in consequence of their transgressions; . . . Therefore, they must needs be chastened and tried, even as Abraham, who was commanded to offer up his only son. . . . Behold, I say unto you, there were jarrings, and contentions, and envyings, and strifes, and lustful and covetous desires among them; therefore by these things they polluted their inheritances. They were slow to hearken unto the voice of the Lord their God; therefore, the Lord their God is slow to hearken unto their prayers, to answer them in the day of their trouble. (Doctrine and Covenants 101:2, 4, 6–7)

The Lord also directed, through a parable of a nobleman and his vineyard, that a group priesthood holders go to Jackson County to redeem Zion.

> And the lord of the vineyard said unto one of his servants: Go and gather together the residue of my servants, and take all the strength of mine house, which are my warriors, my young men, and they that are of middle age also among all my servants, who are the strength of mine house, save those only whom I have appointed to tarry; and go ye straightway unto the land of my vineyard, and redeem my vineyard; for it is mine; I have bought it with money. Therefore, get ye straightway unto

my land; break down the walls of mine enemies; throw down their tower, and scatter their watchmen. (Doctrine and Covenants 101:55–57)

Doctrine and Covenants 102: The First High Council

The Prophet frequently convened temporary councils, or conferences in some instances, for various purposes, including for Church discipline. As the Church grew in size and complexity, the need for standing councils became apparent. In a meeting of priesthood leaders held February 17, 1834, in Joseph's home, he said he "would show the order of councils in ancient days as shown to him by vision." He indicated that "Jerusalem was the seat of the Church Council in ancient days" and that "the apostle, Peter, was the president of the council and held the Keys of the Kingdom of God on the earth [and] was appointed to this office by the voice of the Savior and acknowledged in it by the voice of the Church. He had two men appointed as counsellors with him, and in case Peter was absent, his counsellors could also transact business." With regards to disciplinary councils, Joseph added: "It was not the order of heaven in ancient councils to plead for and against the guilty as in our judicial courts (so called) but that every counsellor when he arose to speak, should speak precisely according to evidence and according to the teaching of the spirit of the Lord."[96]

At this same meeting, Joseph facilitated the initial organization of a standing "Presidents church council."[97] Orson Hyde took the minutes at the meeting. Inasmuch as meeting minutes were meant to establish Church policies and procedures as well as canonize the Doctrine and Covenants, Joseph sought inspiration to revise them; then he presented them to a council of sixty-two priesthood holders and to Church members two days later, at which time they were accepted by unanimous vote. He then provided training and several blessings to the twelve members of the council, adding that "the Council was organized according to the ancient order, and also according to the mind of the Lord."[98]

---

96   Minute Book 1, February 17, 1834, 29–30, JSP.
97   Minute Book 1, February 17, 1834, 29, JSP.
98   Minute Book 1, February 19, 1834, 37, JSP.

The minutes now recorded in Doctrine and Covenants 102 provides some description of the February 17 events as well as the purpose for the council and its original members.

> This day a general council of twenty-four high priests assembled at the house of Joseph Smith, Jun., by revelation, and proceeded to organize the high council of the church of Christ, which was to consist of twelve high priests, and one or three presidents as the case might require. The high council was appointed by revelation for the purpose of settling important difficulties which might arise in the church, which could not be settled by the church or the bishop's council to the satisfaction of the parties. Joseph Smith, Jun., Sidney Rigdon and Frederick G. Williams were acknowledged presidents by the voice of the council; and Joseph Smith, Sen., John Smith, Joseph Coe, John Johnson, Martin Harris, John S. Carter, Jared Carter, Oliver Cowdery, Samuel H. Smith, Orson Hyde, Sylvester Smith, and Luke Johnson, high priests, were chosen to be a standing council for the church, by the unanimous voice of the council. (Doctrine and Covenants 102:1–3)

In effect, this revelation not only established the council but in effect established the Kirtland Stake with the First Presidency as the Kirtland Stake presidency. It also temporarily established the Kirtland Stake high council as a council with general Church authority, a role that was eventually transferred to the Quorum of the Twelve Apostles. It also defined how all high council disciplinary councils were to be held in the future.

The Prophet organized another standing high council in Clay County, Missouri, the following July according to the pattern given in section 102. After most of the Saints in Clay County moved to Caldwell County between 1836 and 1847, this Missouri council continued to function in Far West. When Joseph moved to Far West arriving in March 1838, this Missouri council replaced the Kirtland high council as the "high Council at the seat of the general government of the church."[99]

---

99   Minute Book 1, February 17, 1834, 35, JSP.

Doctrine and Covenants 103: The Redemption of Zion and Zion's Camp

Exactly one week after Joseph Smith organized the first high council, Parley P. Pratt and Lyman Wight, who had traveled from Clay County, Missouri, to Kirtland, made a report to the Kirtland high council about the plight of the Saints who had moved north of Jackson County into Clay County back in November 1833. They asked the council "how and by what means Zion was to be redeemed from our enemies." Joseph had already learned something of Zion's redemption in section 101 through the parable of a nobleman and his vineyard, so it is not surprising that he volunteered to lead an excursion to Missouri and that another thirty or so other brethren volunteered to join him. The council then decided to appoint Joseph as "Commander in chief of the Armies of Israel and the leader of those who volunteered to go."[100] It is unclear whether Joseph's volunteering resulted from him being directed to do so in the revelation now recorded as section 103 or whether the revelation validated his volunteering; the record of section 103 does not conclusively state whether Joseph received the revelation before, during, or after the council meeting.

The revelation now found in Doctrine and Covenants 103 repeats, to a limited extent, the explanations found in section 101 regarding why the mobs were allowed to forcibly remove the Saints from Jackson County: "That those who call themselves after my name might be chastened for a little season with a sore and grievous chastisement, because they did not hearken altogether unto the precepts and commandments which I gave unto them" (verse 4). The Lord also provided additional rationale. Speaking of the mobs, he said: "For I have suffered them thus far, that they might fill up the measure of their iniquities, that their cup might be full" (verse 3). After indicating that "the redemption of Zion must needs come by power" (verse 15), the Lord said that Joseph was "the man to whom [he] likened the servant to whom the Lord of the vineyard spake in the parable which [he had] given unto [him]" (verse 21). He directed Joseph to gather at least one hundred of "the strength of [his] house, [his] young men and the middle aged" (verse 22). But the Lord hoped to gather up to five hundred men "together unto the land of Zion" (verse 22) to "organize [his] kingdom upon the consecrated land and establish the children of Zion" (verse 35). They were going to provide support and protection to the Saints in returning to their lands in Jackson County.

---

100   Minute Book 1, February 24, 1834, 42, JSP.

Eight brethren were directed by the Lord to recruit volunteers and raise funds in companionships—Joseph Smith and Parley P. Pratt, Orson Pratt and Orson Hyde, Hyrum Smith and Frederick G. Williams, and Lyman Wight and Sidney Rigdon. These men acted almost immediately, and after several weeks, their efforts yielded an expedition force of over two hundred men along with some women and children who referred to themselves as the Camp of Israel (now most often referred to as Zion's Camp). The total number was formed by a group from Kirtland led by the Prophet and another from Michigan led by his brother Hyrum. They left in early May 1834 and met up in Salt Creek in eastern Missouri. Not only was the faith of the people in Zion's Camp bolstered by a recognition that they were on the Lord's errand, the Prophet had communicated with Governor Dunkin of Missouri who promised that he would supply a large number of militia to augment the number of Latter-day Saints in the force.

Doctrine and Covenants 105: The Purpose of Zion's Camp

Doctrine and Covenants 105 was not revealed in Joseph Smith's home in Kirtland but rather on Fishing River in western Missouri on June 22, 1834. We have included it in this chapter because it completes the Zion's Camp narrative that began with the revelations revealed in Joseph's Kirtland home (sections 101 and 103). Despite the Lord's direction to provide resources and men and Joseph's constant urging for that support while enroute to Missouri, the eastern Saints mostly ignored the call to arms.

While Joseph's group was at Salt River awaiting the Michigan group, Joseph sent Orson Hyde and Parley P. Pratt to the state capital, Jefferson City, to ascertain whether Governor Dunklin would "fulfill the proposition which he had previously made to the brethren"[101] to provide a military escort that would help the Saints reclaim their lands in Jackson County. Unfortunately, the governor reneged his promise. Governor Dunklin told Orson and Parley that if he were to commit state troops to help them, it might result in "civil war and bloodshed."[102] Joseph recognized that their force was "altogether too small

---

101   Joseph Smith, *History of the Church of Jesus Christ of Latter-day Saints*, ed. B. H. Roberts (Salt Lake City: Deseret Book Company, 1948), 2:88–89.

102   *Autobiography of Parley Parker Pratt, One of the Twelve Apostles of the Church of Jesus Christ of Latter-day Saints, Embracing His Life, Ministry and Travels, with Extracts, in Prose and Verse, from His Miscellaneous Writings*, ed. Parley P. Pratt, 5th ed. (Salt Lake City: Deseret Book, 1961), 115.

for the accomplishment of such a great enterprise,"[103] but his men wanted to press forward and redeem their property in Jackson County regardless.

Before Zion's Camp reached its destination, John J. Ryland of Clay County organized a meeting on June 16 between the Saints in that county and the non-Latter-day Saint residents of Jackson County to negotiate a peaceful reconciliation. The residents offered to buy all of the Saints' land in the county at a price determined by three disinterested mediators on the condition that the Saints would promise to never return. Based on the assumption that the Saints might night agree to their offer, the residents offered an alternate proposal, proposing that the Saints buy all of the property owned by the non-Latter-day Saints in the county at a price determined in the same manner. Neither of these proposals, even if sincere, were amenable to the Saints. The Saints could not afford to purchase all the remaining land, and the Lord had told them not to sell their Jackson County property.

Even though the people in Zion's Camp tried to travel incognito, the people of Missouri were well aware that a military force was heading their way, and reports of its size were grossly overexaggerated. A large number of Missourians had gathered, awaiting the appearance of Zion's Camp, and threatened to attack. On June 19, the camp "intended to enter Clay County . . . but the Lord knew best what was for our good, and so began to hinder our progress. One wheel broke down, another ran off, and one thing after another hindered us so that we had to camp between two forks of Fishing River. If the Camp had not been hindered, they would have crossed into Clay County, and would have been at the mercy of the mob. Thus the Lord, in a marvelous manner, preserved the lives of His servants."[104] The company camped "on an elevated piece of land between Little Fishing and Big Fishing rivers," and Missourians rode into camp, shouting that the Mormons would "'see hell before morning.'"[105] They claimed that three hundred men were on the other side of the Missouri River prepared to attack. While this meeting was taking place, Wilford Woodruff wrote:

> When the five men entered the camp there was not a cloud to be seen in the whole heavens, but as the men left the camp there was a small cloud like a black spot appeared in the north west, and it began to unroll itself like a scroll, and in a few minutes the whole heavens were covered

103   Joseph Smith to Emma Smith, June 4, 1834, 57, JSP.
104   Wilford Woodruff, Journal, 17, M270.1 W893j 197-?, Church History Library, Salt Lake City.
105   Smith, *History of the Church*, 2:103.

with a pall as black as ink. . . . A sudden storm . . . soon broke upon us with wind, rain, thunder and lightning and hail. Our beds were soon afloat and our tents blown down over our heads. We all fled into a Baptist meetinghouse.[106]

As the Prophet Joseph came in shaking the water from his hat and clothing, he said: "Boys, there is some meaning to this. God is in this storm."[107] Joseph recalled:

> The earth trembled and quaked, the rain fell in torrents, and, united, it seemed as if the mandate of vengeance had gone forth from the God of battles, to protect His servants from the destruction of their enemies, for the hail fell on them and not on us, . . . our enemies had holes made in their hats, . . . even the breaking of their rifle stocks, and the fleeing of their horses through fear and pain. . . . In the morning the water in Big Fishing river was about forty feet deep, where, the previous evening, it was no more than to our ankles, and our enemies swore that the water rose thirty feet in thirty minutes in Little Fishing river. They reported that one of their men was killed by lightning, and that another had his hand torn off by his horse drawing his hand between the logs of a corn crib. . . . They declared that if that was the way God fought for the Mormons, they might as well go about their business.[108]

The next day three members of the Ray County militia, including Colonel John Sconce, rode into Zion's Camp to ascertain the plans of the camp. Colonel Sconce said, "'I see that there is an Almighty power that protects this people.'" Joseph explained that they "had come one thousand miles to assist [their] brethren, to bring them clothing, etc., and to reinstate them upon their own land; and that [Zion's Camp] had no intention to molest or injure any people, but only to administer to the wants of [their] afflicted friends; and that the evil reports circulated about [them] were false, and got up by [their] enemies to procure [their] destruction."[109] The three men were so moved by the tales depicting the unjust treatment of the Jackson County Saints that they

106 Wilford Woodruff, as quoted in Marlene C. Kettley, Arnold K. Garr, and Craig K. Manscill, "Zion's Camp," in *Mormon Thoroughfare: A History of the Church in Illinois, 1830–39* (Provo, UT: Brigham Young University Religious Studies Center, 2006), 43–62.

107 Smith, *History of the Church*, 2:104n8.

108 Smith, *History of the Church*, 2:104–5.

109 Smith, *History of the Church*, 2:105.

promised to present the Saints' side of what happened. Despite this expression of positive intent, one citizen of Lexington County, Missouri, wrote: "Should they cross the river [into Jackson County] there will be a battle, and probably much blood shed."[110]

The Prophet was apparently undeterred, and Charles C. Rich wrote in his journal that it was "decided that we should go on armed and equiped."[111] However, on the following day, June 21, several men from Clay and Ray counties, led by Sheriff Cornelius Gilliam, met with camp leaders to warn them of the general panic Zion's Camp had created amongst the citizens of western Missouri. To reduce tensions, Joseph and other leaders signed a statement promising that the camp did not intend "to commence hostilities against any man or body of men,"[112] that they were willing to negotiate a peaceful settlement. They even proposed that the Saints be allowed to purchase the land of Jackson County residents who were not willing to remain in the county if the Saints returned, apparently unaware of the June 16 negotiations.

The following day, June 22, a council was held "to determine what steps"[113] the camp should take. During the council, the Prophet received the revelation now found in Doctrine and Covenants 105. The Lord began this revelation by reiterating reasons for the Saints' expulsion from Jackson County, reasons he listed in sections 101 and 103: "Behold, I say unto you, were it not for the transgressions of my people, speaking concerning the church and not individuals, they might have been redeemed even now. But behold, they have not learned to be obedient to the things which I required at their hands, but are full of all manner of evil, and do not impart of their substance, as becometh saints, to the poor and afflicted among them" (verses 1–2).

The Lord added to this rationale a problem associated with the lack of support for Zion's Camp from outlying branches, both in terms of personnel and monetary resources: "But I speak concerning my churches abroad—there are many who will say: Where is their God? Behold, he will deliver them in time of trouble, otherwise we will not go up unto Zion, and will keep our moneys. . . . Behold, I have commanded my servant Joseph Smith, Jun., to say unto the strength . . . to gather together for the redemption of my people, . . . but the strength of mine house have not hearkened unto my words" (verses 8, 16–17).

---

110   "The Mormon Controversy," *Daily National Intelligencer*, July 23, 1834.

111   Charles C. Rich, Diaries, July 1–December 21, 1834, MS 13083, Church History Library, Salt Lake City.

112   Declaration, June 21, 1834, [1], JSP.

113   *Autobiography of William Farrington Cahoon* (Salt Lake City: Paragon Press, 1960), http://boap.org/LDS/Early-Saints/WFCahoon.html.

On June 25, Joseph divided Zion's Camp into several small groups to show the Missouri citizenry that the camp did not intend to harm anyone. The following week, on July 3, Joseph directed Lyman Wight to honorably discharge "every man of the Camp who had proved himself faithful."[114] Lyman recorded, "[Joseph] further said that he was now willing to return home, that he was fully satisfied that he had done the will of God, and that the Lord had accepted our sacrifice and offering, even as he had Abraham's when he offered his son Isaac; and in his benediction asked the heavenly Father to bless us with eternal life and salvation."[115]

After camp members heard the revelation, some accepted it as "the word of the lord" and "rejoiced."[116] Nathan Baldwin described it as "the most acceptable to [him] of anything [he] had ever heard before, the gospel being the exception."[117] However, not all camp members reacted as Nathan did. "Many in the camp murmured because [they] were not permitted at this time to restore [their] brethren at all hazards."[118]

As the camp was disbanding, about seventy were hit with cholera. A few weeks prior, Joseph had expressed concern about "the fractious and unruly spirits" in the camp, and stated that God had shown him a great scourge that would afflict the camp, making them "die like sheep with the rot." Joseph said repentance and humility would reduce the extent of the scourge, but the Lord would not totally protect the camp on account of them "giving way to their unruly temper."[119] Several camp members saw the cholera outbreak as the scourge the Prophet referred to. Wilford Woodruff remarked, "Brother Joseph prophesied that . . . a scourge awaited the camp and as it was prophesied of so it was fulfilled. For soon after we had camped . . . we were visited by the destroying angel."[120]

---

114   Smith, *History of the Church*, 2:123.

115   *History of the Church of Jesus Christ of Latter Day Saints* (Lamoni, IA: Reorganized Church of Jesus Christ of Latter Day Saints, 1897), 1:515–16, http://www.center-place.org/history/ch/v1ch18.htm.

116   Joseph Bates Noble, Reminiscences, circa 1836, MS 1031, Church History Library, Salt Lake City.

117   Nathan Baldwin, Account of Zion's Camp, 1882, MS 499, typescript, Church History Library, Salt Lake City.

118   *Autobiography of William Farrington Cahoon.*

119   "Extracts from H. C. Kimball's Journal," *The Times and Seasons* 6, no. 2 (February 1, 1845): 788.

120   Scott G. Kenney, ed., *Wilford Woodruff's Journal* (Midvale, UT: Signature Books, 1983), 1:12.

Doctrine and Covenants 104: The United Firm

In the midst of the Missouri difficulties on April 23, 1834, and prior to the Zion's Camp march, the Lord revealed his will concerning reorganizing the United Firm. This organization had been formed in April 1832 as an extension of the law of consecration to manage the Church's mercantile and publishing endeavors and had served as an important administrative structure since that time (see Doctrine and Covenants 78:3; 82:11–12). The United Firm consisted of two mercantile companies and one literary company: the Newel K. Whitney and Sidney Gilbert store in Kirtland, Ohio, originally created in 1826; the Gilbert, Whitney & Co. Store, a company created after Sidney was commanded to move to Missouri in early 1832; and the Literary Firm, which consisted of six men called to manage Church publications (see Doctrine and Covenants 70), specifically W. W. Phelps & Co in Missouri and F. G. Williams & Co. in Kirtland. The members of the United Firm were Joseph Smith, Sidney Rigdon, Oliver Cowdery, John Whitmer, William W. Phelps, Martin Harris, Edward Partridge, Newel K. Whitney, Sidney Gilbert, Frederick G. Williams, and John Johnson, all of whom had consecrated property to the Church.

At the time of the revelation now found in Doctrine and Covenants 104, the United Firm faced substantial financial and spiritual challenges. Mobs in Missouri destroyed the Church printing press in July 1833, effectively eliminating the ability of W. W. Phelps & Co. to discharge the debts it incurred during its initial creation. Also, members of the United Firm who lived in Kirtland were heavily indebted to N. K. Whitney & Co., resulting in the latter becoming indebted to companies in the east in order to acquire store goods. Lastly, two firm members, William W. Phelps and Sidney Gilbert, may have been the reason why the Lord said in this revelation that "some of [his] servants have not kept the commandment but have broken the covenant through covetousness" (verse 4). Sidney had apparently refused to provide help for some of the poor in Missouri who deserved it, and William used language in describing the printing press in Missouri and its products as belonging to him.

With the extreme stress Zion's Camp would place on Church finances, particularly without the support the Lord expected Church branches to provide, members of the United Firm in Kirtland met on April 10, 1834, and agreed "that the firm should be dissolved and each one"[121] receive a stewardship, business, or property to manage. In response, the Lord said that the firm

121   Joseph Smith, Journal, April 10, 1834, JSP.

should "appoint every man his stewardship" (verse 11), agreeing with the firm's decision but expounding that it should not be dissolved but rather reorganized with the two branches in Missouri and Kirtland separated (see verses 48–50).

Remarkably, the property and other holdings granted as stewardships came from the unselfish consecrations of three members of the United Firm—Newel K. Whitney, Frederick G. Williams, and John Johnson. In other words, the personal property or funds obtained from the sale of the personal property of just three men provided the stewardships for the eleven members of the firm.

Doctrine and Covenants 106: Warren Cowdery

The revelation now found in Doctrine and Covenants 106 was meant for Warren Cowdery, the older brother of Oliver Cowdery. Although he was Oliver's brother and was somewhat sympathetic to the Saints, it was not until the summer of 1834 that he was baptized. Around the time of his baptism in his home in Freedom, New York, where there existed a branch of the Church, Warren wrote to Oliver indicating that "a preacher of [their] order" would "do [the Freedom Branch] good, by strengthening and building [them] up in the most holy faith."[122] He wrote Oliver again a month later, having "had thoughts of requesting [Oliver] to enquire what is the will of the Lord concerning [him]," hoping that he could be "useful in the vineyard of the Lord."[123] Both of Warren's requests were answered in this revelation. The Lord said, "It is my will that my servant Warren A. Cowdery should be appointed and ordained a presiding high priest over my church, in the land of Freedom and the regions round about" (verse 1). The Lord then expressed joy in Warren's humility and initial conversion: "And again, verily I say unto you, there was joy in heaven when my servant Warren bowed to my scepter, and separated himself from the crafts of men" (verse 6). He then promised blessings "notwithstanding the vanity of his heart," saying: "I will lift him up inasmuch as he will humble himself before me" (verse 7).

Warren presided over the Freedom Branch until he moved his family to Kirtland early in 1836 where he served the Church as a scribe and recorder.

---

122 Warren Cowdery to Oliver Cowdery, September 1, 1834, in *The Evening and the Morning Star*, September 24, 1834, 189.

123 Warren Cowdery to Oliver Cowdery, October, 28, 1834, in *LDS Messenger and Advocate*, November 1834, 1:22.

Unfortunately, Warren did not "continue to be a faithful witness and a light unto the church" (verse 8), but rather he got caught up in the difficulties around the Kirtland Safety Society and fought against the Prophet in 1837–38.

Ordination of Oliver Cowdery as Assistant President and an Unpublished Revelation

Image of Oliver Cowdery.
Courtesy Joseph Smith Papers.

On the evening of December 5, 1834, Joseph Smith's counselors, Sidney Rigdon and Frederick G. Williams, joined him for the purpose of ordaining Oliver Cowdery as Assistant President of the Church, or as Oliver recorded it: "Assistant President of the High and Holy Priesthood in the Church of the Latter-Day Saints." Oliver contrasted his office with that of Joseph's saying that the Assistant President is "to assist in presiding over the whole church, and to officiate in the absence of the President, according to his rank and appointment."[124] He then listed the seniority in the First Presidency: Joseph Smith, Oliver Cowdery, Sidney Rigdon, Frederick G. Williams.

Oliver went to explain why this restructuring did not occur sooner, indicating that he remained in Missouri following his mission to the Lamanites (see Doctrine and Covenants 28) "to assist Wm W. Phelps in conducting the printing business; but that this promise [of his station in Church hierarchy] was made by the angel while in company with President Smith, at the time

---

124   Account of Meetings, Revelation, and Blessing, December 5–6, 1834, 17, JSP.

they received the office of the lesser priesthood."[125] Thus, "the circumstances and situation of the Church"[126] required that Sidney and Frederick be ordained before Oliver.

It was after this ordination was conducted that Joseph received a revelation—not published or canonized—that comprised a rebuke for the First Presidency: "Verily, condemnation resteth upon you, who are appointed to lead my church, and to be saviors of men: and also upon the church: And there must needs be a repentance and a reformation among you, in all things, in your ensamples before the church, and before the world, in all your manners, habits and customs, and salutations one toward another rendering unto every man the respect due the office, calling, and priesthood, whereunto I the Lord have appointed and ordained you. Amen."[127]

Doctrine and Covenants 107: A Revelation on Priesthood[128]

The revelation now found in Doctrine and Covenants 107 is actually an inspired compilation of five revelations Joseph Smith received around April 1835 before the Church published the first edition of the Doctrine and Covenants. During a twelve-day period in November 1831 in the Hiram, Ohio, home of John and Elsa Johnson, the Prophet received eight revelations. One of these, received on November 11, was a revelation dealing with organizational structures in Church administration and the responsibilities associated with quorum leadership. The exact context for the revelation is unknown, but historical records do indicate that Reynolds Cahoon's question of whether he should travel to Missouri in the following spring was discussed in a conference of elders held on that day. Besides discussing Reynolds's question, Oliver Cowdery

---

125   Account of Meetings, Revelation, and Blessing, December 5–6, 1834, 17, JSP.
      The Joseph Smith Papers editors added this explanation regarding what John the
      Baptist said: "JS later recounted that he and Cowdery received the lesser priest-
      hood from John the Baptist on 15 May 1829 and that the angelic visitor instructed
      that Cowdery be made second elder, next to JS as first elder. JS and Cowdery were
      acknowledged in these positions at the organization of the church. (JS History,
      vol. A-1, 17–18; Articles and Covenants, ca. Apr. 1830, in Doctrine and Covenants
      2:1, 1835 ed. [D&C 20:2–3].)."
126   Account of Meetings, Revelation, and Blessing, December 5–6, 1834, 17, JSP.
127   Account of Meetings, Revelation, and Blessing, December 5–6, 1834, 17, JSP.
128   Authors' note: Much of the content in these paragraphs on section 107 was tak-
      en from the book *The Voice of the Lord is Unto All Men: A Remarkable Year of
      Revelations in the Johnson Home*, written by the authors.

read "commandments concerning the duties of the Elders,"[129] during which this revelation may have also been received. It now appears as verses 58–100 of section 107 and includes inspired changes that were made to some of the verses while the Prophet was preparing the revelations for publication in the 1835 Doctrine and Covenants.

This 1831 revelation contains an allusion to the "church laws respecting church business" (verse 59). These laws probably include the three revelations known as the "Articles and Covenants," most of which were given around April 6, 1830, in the Peter Sr. and Mary Whitmer home in Fayette, New York (Doctrine and Covenants 20), the "Laws of the Church of Christ" given on February 9 and 23, 1831 in the Newel K. and Elizabeth Ann Whitney home in Kirtland (Doctrine and Covenants 42), and a portion of a revelation given November 1, 1831 in the Johnson home (Doctrine and Covenants 68:13–24), ten days prior to the reception of this portion of section 107.

These revelations comprise about half of the latter verses of section 107, and the circumstances surrounding the reception of the first half are indicative of the revelatory process surrounding the Prophet's preparation of the revelations for the first edition of the Doctrine and Covenants. In March 1835, a month after the Quorum of the Twelve Apostles was first organized, the First Presidency and the Twelve decided that the Twelve should travel to the eastern branches and conduct a series of local conferences. These conferences were to be held "for the purpose of regulateing all things necessary"[130] in response to "the many pressing requests from the eastern churches."[131] To prepare the Twelve for this mission, Joseph presented to them a compilation of revelations that was later entitled "On Priesthood"; it was numbered as section 3 in the 1835 edition of the Doctrine and Covenants and is currently numbered as section 107. It comprises one of the premier sections outlining doctrines of the priesthood and the structures of priesthood organizations. It also represents the inspired interweaving of two 1835 revelatory recordings, inspired insights contributed by the Prophet, the 1831 revelation, and two unpublished revelations. One such revelation detailing responsibilities of the bishop was revealed in mid-March 1832 in the Johnson home, and the other was probably received in January 1833 calling Frederick G. Williams to replace Jesse Gause as a counselor to the Prophet.[132] This compilation of revelations provides doc-

---

129   Minutes, November 11, 1831, JSP.
130   Record of the Twelve, February 14–August 28, 1835, 4, The Joseph Smith Papers .
131   "Historical Introduction," Instruction on Priesthood, between circa March 1 and circa May 4, 1835 [D&C 107], JSP.
132   "Historical Introduction," Revelation, January 5, 1833, JSP.

trinal insights about the priesthood beyond what had already been revealed, and it includes important clarifications and elaborations on the government of the Church, such as explanations of the duties of Church officers.[133]

Egyptian Mummies and the Book of Abraham

A fragment of some of the papyri associated with the Book of Abraham. Courtesy Joseph Smith Papers.

In July 1835, Joseph Smith, with the financial assistance of a few other Saints in Kirtland, purchased four ancient Egyptian mummies and a number

---

133   Verses 53–55 regarding Adam-ondi-Ahman are of special interest. They describe a meeting of Adam with his righteous posterity in the valley of Adam-ondi-Ahman. It has been thought that these verses were revealed on December 18, 1833, while Joseph ordained his father as the first Church patriarch in the Johnson Inn in Kirtland (Joseph Fielding Smith, ed., *Teachings of the Prophet Joseph Smith* [Salt Lake City: Deseret Book, 1976], 38). However, although Joseph Smith Sr. did receive a blessing of some sort that day along with several others, he was not ordained a patriarch until a year later, December 6, 1834, when he was also ordained "Assistant President of the Church of the Latter-day Saints" (Blessing from Joseph Smith Sr., December 9, 1834, JSP. It is now known these words were part of the 1835 section "On Priesthood." Interestingly, in September 1835, when Oliver Cowdery recorded the 1833 blessings in his patriarchal blessing book, he added these "words which fell from his [Joseph's] lips while the visions of the Almighty were open to his view" (Appendix 5: Blessings, September and October 1835, Introduction, JSP, thus adding to the list of appearances of deity to the Prophet that occurred in Kirtland.

of papyrus scrolls from an antiquities dealer named Michael Chandler. The mummies and the papyri most likely came from tombs exhumed near the ancient Egyptian city of Thebes in the early decades of the nineteenth century by an Italian antiquities dealer named Antonio Lebolo. Antonio's expeditions to Egypt came as part of a general excitement over Egyptian antiquities caused by the expeditions of Napoleon Bonaparte into the region in the late eighteenth and early nineteenth centuries. Sometime between 1817 and 1821, Antonio unearthed a tomb holding a large collection of mummies and papyri.[134] After Antonio's death in 1830, his estate and his Egyptian collection made its way to the United States where it became part of a traveling exhibition shown in nearly a dozen cities throughout the country.[135]

Michael's exact relationship to Antonio and the collection are not fully known, but he had been referred to Joseph as a person who could perhaps translate the ancient characters on the papyri. A letter from W. W. Phelps, one of Joseph's close associates, captures the excitement in Kirtland surrounding the papyri: "On the last of June four Egyptian mummies were brought here. With them were two papyrus rolls, besides some other ancient Egyptian writings. . . . They were presented to President Smith. He soon knew what they were and said that the rolls of papyrus contained a sacred record kept by Joseph in Pharaoh's court in Egypt and the teachings of Father Abraham. . . . These records of old times when we translate and print them in a book will make a good witness for the Book of Mormon."

In the fall of 1835, after purchasing the mummies and papyri, Joseph and his scribes began translating the ancient Egyptian materials. Joseph's journal from October to December 1835 contains nine entries related to the translation work carried out on these texts. A typical entry from November 19, 1835, reads: "I returned home and spent the day in translating the Egyptian records." The text produced by the Prophet during this period is a remarkable account of the early life of the biblical patriarch Abraham. The work recontextualizes Abraham as an early witness of Jesus Christ. It provides some of the most valuable teachings known on the premortal nature of humanity and the selection of Christ as the Savior of God's children. It also includes a new account of the creation of the earth, detailing how the Creation was planned before it was

134 Book of Abraham and Related Manuscripts, JSP.
135 Brent M. Rogers, Elizabeth A. Kuehn, Christian K. Heimburger, Max H Parkin, Alexander L. Baugh, and Steven C. Harper, eds., *Documents, Volume 5: October 1835–January 1838*, vol. 5 of Documents series of *The Joseph Smith Papers*, ed. Ronald K. Esplin, Matthew J. Grow, and Matthew C. Godfrey (Salt Lake City: Church Historian's Press, 2017) 71–72.

carried out. Perhaps most poignantly, the account explains how Abraham—a man most known for having his faith tested by God asking him to sacrifice his son—was nearly sacrificed himself as a young man by his wicked father. The translation was published in the *Times and Seasons* in Nauvoo in 1842 with an introduction that read "'A translation Of some ancient Records that have fallen into our hands, from the Catecombs of Egypt, purporting to be the writings of Abraham, while he was in Egypt, called the BOOK OF ABRAHAM, written by his own hand, upon papyrus.'"[136] The Book of Abraham was canonized in 1880. In addition to translating the first-person narrative of the life of Abraham, Joseph and his scribes also worked on producing some Egyptian alphabet and grammar texts.

Doctrine and Covenants 134: A Statement on Government

In August 1835, the newly published Doctrine and Covenants was presented to the Church in Kirtland for a sustaining vote by Oliver Cowdery and Sidney Rigdon. Joseph Smith and his second counselor, Frederick G. Williams, were in Michigan and so were not present at the time. After the sustaining, William W. Phelps and Oliver called upon the congregation to "accept and adopt" two other documents: a statement on marriage and a declaration on government and law. The latter now appears in the Doctrine and Covenants as section 134. Although its authorship is uncertain, subsequent statements of the Prophet suggests he approved of it, at least eventually. He may not have known Oliver was going to present it or the statement on marriage. On the other hand, because the statement on marriage forbade polygamy, Joseph never sanctioned it.

Doctrine and Covenants 108: Revelation for Lyman Sherman

As a newly called president of the Seventy, Lyman Sherman asked the Prophet on December 26, 1835, to inquire of the Lord for a revelation that "should make known [his] duty."[137] Lyman was an 1832 convert from New York who brought his family to Kirtland in 1833. He, like all the other Seventies presidents and most of the Quorum of the Twelve, marched with

136   Book of Abraham and Egyptian Material, JSP.
137   Joseph Smith, Journal, December 26, 1835, JSP.

Zion's Camp. It appears his request was divinely inspired because the Lord stated: "Your sins are forgiven you, because you have obeyed my voice in coming up hither this morning to receive counsel of him whom I have appointed" (verse 1). The counsel and direction he received included an oft-quoted verse about how the Saints should conduct themselves. "Therefore, strengthen your brethren in all your conversation, in all your prayers, in all your exhortations, and in all your doings" (verse 7).

Joseph Smith Store

The remnants of the Joseph Smith Kirtland Store in 2018, prior to its restoration. Photo by Casey Paul Griffiths.

To augment his income, Joseph Smith opened a variety store across the street east from his home which he supplied with goods he acquired while on a trip to New York. Unfortunately, it was difficult for him to make a profit because he extended credit when asked. His busy schedule precluded him from being able to manage the daily operations of the store, so he hired others, including Ira Ames, to help. The store was only open less than a year—Joseph closed it so as to avoid offending Church members.

In a 1852 discourse, Brigham Young explained some of the challenges the Joseph faced acting as the proprietor of the store and the Prophet of the Lord at the same time:

> Joseph goes to New York and buys 20,000 dollars' worth of goods, comes into Kirtland and commences to trade. In comes one of the brethren, "Brother Joseph, let me have a frock pattern for my wife." What if Joseph says, "No, I cannot without the money." The consequences would be, "He is no Prophet," says James. Pretty soon Thomas walks in. "Brother Joseph, will you trust me for a pair of boots?" "No, I cannot let them go without the money." "Well," says Thomas, "Brother Joseph is no Prophet; I have found that out, and I am glad of it."

Brigham continued:

> After awhile, in comes Bill and sister Susan. Says Bill, "Brother Joseph, I want a shawl, I have not got the money, but I wish you to trust me a week or a fortnight." Well, Brother Joseph thinks the others have gone and apostatized, and he don't know but these goods will make the whole Church do the same, so he lets Bill have a shawl. Bill walks off with it and meets a brother. "Well," says he, "what do you think of brother Joseph?" "O he is a first-rate man, and I fully believe he is a Prophet. See here, he has trusted me this shawl." Richard says, "I think I will go down and see if he won't trust me some." In walks Richard. "Brother Joseph, I want to trade about 20 dollars." "Well," says Joseph, "these goods will make the people apostatize, so over they go, they are of less value than the people." Richard gets his goods. Another comes in the same way to make a trade of 25 dollars, and so it goes.
>
> Joseph was a first-rate fellow with them all the time, provided he never would ask them to pay him. In this way it is easy for us to trade away a first-rate store of goods, and be in debt for them. . . . I have known persons that would have cursed brother Joseph to the lowest hell hundreds of times, because he would not trust out everything he had on the face of the earth, and let the people squander it to the four winds. When he had let many of the brethren and sisters have goods on trust, he could not meet his liabilities, and then they would turn round and say, "What is the matter brother Joseph, why don't you pay your debts?" "It is quite a curiosity that you don't pay your debts; you must be a bad financier; you don't know how to handle the things of this world." At the same time the coats, pants, dresses, boots and shoes that they and their families were

wearing came out of Joseph's store, and were not paid for when they were cursing him for not paying his debts.[138]

Leaving Kirtland

This chapter includes only a sample of events and revelations that occurred while Joseph and Emma Smith and their family lived in the only home they owned in Kirtland. As in all the other locations where Joseph lived, his Kirtland home was made sacred by the revelations he received there. Following the collapse of the Kirtland Safety Society in 1837, intense persecution and threats on his life prompted Joseph to immediately reply to a revelation he received on January 12, 1838, to leave Kirtland. Sidney Rigdon and Joseph left that night, and their families soon joined them en route to Far West, Missouri.

Mini-Devotional—Waiting on the Lord

Joseph Smith was living in his Kirtland home while he dealt with the persecutions of the Saints in Jackson County, Missouri. When he received word that the Saints had been driven from Jackson County, he asked the Lord for the reason, but it took a few months before the Lord answered. Faith in the Lord includes faith in his timing.

- Discuss times in your individual life or in the life of your family where you have had to "wait upon the Lord."

---

138   Richard S. Van Wagoner, ed., *The Complete Discourses of Brigham Young* (Salt Lake City: Smith-Pettit Foundation, 2009), p. 601, 1017.

Significant events at this location:

- The Lord commanded the Saints in Kirtland to build a "house of prayer, a house of fasting, a house of faith, a house of learning, a house of glory, a house of order, a house of God" (Doctrine and Covenants 88:119).

- The Kirtland Temple was one of three houses designated in revelation that the Saints were asked to build. The other houses were a house for the presidency and a house for the printing of the scriptures (Doctrine and Covenants 94).

- At the dedication of the temple on March 27, 1836, the hosanna shout was performed by the Saints for the first time, and Joseph Smith read the dedicatory prayer (Doctrine and Covenants 109).

- Emma Smith completed a hymn book for the dedication of the temple (see Doctrine and Covenants 25:11–12). Among the hymns included was "The Spirit of God" by W. W. Phelps, which was sung for the first time during the dedication.

- In the weeks leading up to the dedication of the temple, Joseph Smith was shown a vision wherein he saw his deceased brother, Alvin, in the celestial kingdom.

- Joseph Smith and Oliver Cowdery witnessed an appearance of Jesus Christ in the temple on April 3, 1836. The ancient prophets Moses, Elias, and Elijah bestowed priesthood keys upon Joseph and Oliver at this time.

- A financial crisis in 1837 caused many Church members to apostatize. During this time, many Saints, including Joseph Smith and his family, left Kirtland. Ownership of the Kirtland Temple was given to the forbears of Community of Christ when they occupied the temple in the late nineteenth century.

THE KIRTLAND TEMPLE

The Kirtland temple, dedicated in 1836, was the hearth of the Latter-day Saint community in Kirtland. Photo by Acacia E. Griffiths.

The Kirtland Temple is a magnificent structure with a history so rich that no written record of its history can even begin to scratch the surface. Currently, Community of Christ[139] owns the temple, the property it sits on, and a beautiful visitors' center next door. More important, they have been and continue

---

139 Community of Christ was formerly known as The Reorganized Church of Jesus Christ of Latter Day Saints. Community of Christ was founded in 1852 by Jason Briggs, William Marks, and Zenos Gurley. In 1860, Joseph Smith III became president of the church. The church formally changed its name to Community of Christ in 2001. Though Community of Christ and The Church of Jesus Christ of Latter-day Saints have a shared heritage and some beliefs are common, they have also developed separately for nearly two centuries and have many differences in their doctrine.

to be very faithful stewards of this sacred building, and thanks be to God for their sacrifice and long-term commitment to its preservation. No trip to Kirtland is complete without touring the temple. This chapter will pick up where the chapter on the Whitney Store left off regarding the construction, dedication, and use of the Kirtland Temple in the 1830s. It will also touch on the Stannard Quarry (where workers obtained much of the stone for the temple's construction), the printing office that used to stand next to the temple, and the Kirtland cemetery which sits just north of the temple.

Temple Construction

The Church purchased the one-hundred-acre Peter French Farm in April 1833 for $5,000, and part of the property was designated as the temple site. Two thousand dollars was paid as a down payment, and the purchase agreement called for the balance to be paid in installments within two years. Some payments were made, but the Church fell behind. Foreclosure was imminent. Following a spiritual impression, John Tanner, a wealthy convert from New York, moved his family to Kirtland in 1835 and loaned the Prophet $2,000 ($61,000 by today's standards) to help pay off the temple debt. John later loaned the temple committee $13,000 and then signed a note for another $30,000, none of which was ever repaid.

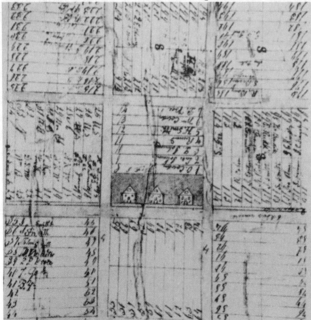

Detail of the plan for Kirtland, with a House for the Presidency, a House for the Printing of the Scriptures, and a House of the Lord. Courtesy Joseph Smith Papers.

On June 1, 1833, the Lord rebuked the Saints for only dedicating minimal effort to building the temple (see Doctrine and Covenants 95). The Saints repented and made a concerted and sustained effort that commenced June 5 and culminated in the completed temple nearly three years later. Hyrum Smith and Reynolds Cahoon, two members of the temple building committee, sought to be first to commence the construction. Hyrum cut down the existing Smith wheat crop on the property designated for the temple site, and he was the first to begin digging the foundation. He was soon joined by Reynolds and others who dug the entire 15,000-square-foot foundation by hand. On the same day, George A. Smith, Joseph Smith's fifteen-year-old cousin, and Harvey Stanley delivered the first load of sandstone to the temple site. On July 23, the Saints performed a ceremony in conjunction with laying the four cornerstones, and young George had to be ordained a high priest in order to have a sufficient number of brethren holding that office to conduct the ceremony. The foundation was four feet thick with large stone blocks on the outside and irregular rubble stone cemented together on the inside. Thanks to the work of almost every available man, the foundation walls rose to a height of four feet above ground level by September. Rough-hewn lumber spanned the foundation as floor joists.

Walls above the foundation were intended to be made of brick. Unfortunately, the bricks crumbled when fired, causing a temporary construction suspension. Responding to a letter of invitation from Hyrum Smith, Artemus Millet, a recent convert and expert stonemason from Canada, arrived about this time and suggested using the local rough-cut sandstone to complete the foundation and construct the walls. This method was well known in parts of Canada, and it provided a faster and less expensive means of building the walls. Upon completing the rough-stone construction, stucco would be added to the exterior.

As the construction increased in the fall and winter, so did opposition from early Kirtland residents. Threats to the safety of the workmen, Church leaders, and the temple itself were frequent. Guards were posted at night and some men did not remove their work clothes and slept with their rifles for weeks at a time.

Interior of the Kirtland Temple walls show the rubble stone construction. Stucco was added to the exterior of the walls to provide a uniform appearance. Photo by Casey Paul Griffiths, courtesy Community of Christ.

Another significant slowdown in construction commenced in May 1834 when Zion's Camp led one hundred and thirty of the most able-bodied men to Missouri, along with most of the resources possessed by the impoverished Saints. Joseph Smith Sr. and Sidney Rigdon led the approximately fifteen men left behind to continue the construction. Heber C. Kimball reported that Sidney "frequently used to go upon the walls of the building both by night and day and frequently wetting the walls with his tears, crying aloud to the Almighty to send means whereby [they] might accomplish the building."[140] The men in Zion's Camp were discharged in late June 1834, and by fall, nearly fifty men could be seen laboring together as carpenters, painters, joiners, masons, or mortar makers. Brigham Young reported that he and "Joseph Smith . . . worked on that building day after day; also, many others did so. They did not have molasses to eat with their johnny cake. Sometimes they had shoes, and sometimes, not; sometimes they would have tolerable pants, and, sometimes, very ragged ones."[141]

---

140   "Extracts from H. C. Kimball's Journal," *Times and Seasons* 6, no. 7 (April 15, 1845): 867.

141   Marba C. Josephson, "Romance of Temple Building," *Improvement Era,* April 1950.

February 1835 saw the walls completed and the commencement of the roof, which took another five months to complete. The height of the temple required interlocking cornerstones, or "quoins," to strengthen the walls. The exterior windows were installed within stones—not wood—casements, and all of the windows were cut and installed by Brigham and Joseph Young in November 1835. Their brother, Lorenzo, joined Artemus Millet in supervising the stucco work on the exterior, which had ground crockery and glass—obtained from trash heaps—added to it to increase its luster and blue lines drawn upon it by Joseph Young to provide an appearance of masonry.

Jacob Bump supervised the interior plastering, which also began in November 1835 along with the interior finishing woodwork on the main floor, or "lower court." Wood "fluting," a form of ornamental carving, adorned the walls, columns, and ceiling of the temple. Truman Angell utilized a simpler "fretwork" patterning using think wood strips to ornament the second "upper court." Interior painting supervised by Brigham Young began in February 1836 on the third floor. Emma Smith and Joseph Smith Sr. directed the sisters in sewing carpets and curtains, or "veils," for the temple. The sisters also provided food and clothing for the workmen, and some even provided manual labor when most the men were away with Zion's Camp.

Spiritual Manifestations Prior to the Dedication

The temple was dedicated in March 1836, and those in attendance recorded many marvelous spiritual experiences. Additionally, in the weeks leading up to the temple dedication, several members recorded many miraculous spiritual manifestations surrounding the temple. Table 1 provides details of some of the more major miracles and spiritual manifestations that occurred in January and February 1836. In January, Roger Orton saw angels on fiery horses surrounding temple. Note that in some instances, who it was that actually saw these manifestations is not entirely clear. On January 21, when the first initiatory ordinances were being sealed for the First Presidency, the Missouri stake presidency, and the two bishoprics, six separate visions were seen, including multiple visions of members of the Godhead. One of these visions is recorded in Doctrine and Covenants 137. The next day, the Quorum of the Twelve and the Seventies presidents gathered with the First Presidency for the same reason and were joined by angels as they sang hymns. The following day, the Joseph Smith was joined by others to perform the ordinance of the washing of feet, and some were heard to sing with the gift of tongues. On January 28, while hundreds of brethren met in priesthood quorums, Joseph beheld another vision of the Father and the Son.

Table 1. Spiritual manifestations in the Kirtland Temple, January through February 1836

Date (1836)	Circumstance	Who was there (and saw?)		What was seen
January	(guarding temple)	Roger Orton	•	Six angels on fiery horses surrounding temple
January 21	(washing), anointing, sealing anointing	Joseph Smith, First Presidency, Missouri Stake presidency, Missouri and Ohio bishoprics, scribe (last vision—Missouri and Kirtland high councils)	•	Father and Son, Adam, Abraham, Smith family
			•	Twelve Apostles in foreign lands, Son of God
			•	Twelve Apostles, Adam, Father and Son, throne in celestial kingdom
			•	McLellin healing, Young foreign tongue
			•	(all brethren saw?) Twelve Apostles in celestial kingdom, Father and Son?, legions of angels, temple filled with glory, protection
			•	Son of God
January 22	Anointing, sealing anointing	Joseph Smith, First Presidency, Twelve Apostles, Seven presidents of the Seventies	•	Angels singing with brethren
January 23	Washing of feet	Joseph Smith and others	•	Singing in tongues
January 28	Hundreds of brethren in priesthood quorums	Joseph Smith	•	Father and Son
February 6			•	Visions
			•	Prophesying

The Temple Dedication

The Kirtland Temple. Photo by Casey Paul Griffiths.

On Sunday, March 27, 1836, at the temple dedication, Eliza R. Snow wrote: "The ceremonies of that dedication may be rehearsed, but no mortal language can describe the heavenly manifestations of that memorable day. Angels appeared to some, while a sense of divine presence was realized by all present, and each heart was filled with 'joy inexpressible and full of glory.'"[142] When the First Presidency arrived at 7 a.m., a congregation had already begun to assemble. The First Presidency, doorkeepers, and donations stewards, who later collected $963, entered the temple and dedicated the pulpits. By the time the doors opened to the public at 8 a.m., the gathered crowd was approaching 2,000 people. Although the temple was designed to hold between 400 and 500 people, nearly 1,000 were permitted to enter. Needless to say, every space was utilized, including the pulpit boxes, pew boxes, choir boxes, and even the aisles. The Prophet Joseph Smith invited those who were unable to attend to

---

142   Edward W. Tullidge, *The Women of Mormondom* (New York, 1877), 95.

hold their own meetings in the red schoolhouse and in members' homes if needed, promising that another dedication meeting would be held.

The meeting began at 9 a.m. and lasted until well after 4 p.m. with only one intermission. No one moved during that intermission except a few nursing mothers. Sidney Rigdon read Psalms 96 and 24, the latter including these verses: "Who shall ascend into the hill of the Lord? or who shall stand in his holy place? He that hath clean hands, and a pure heart; who hath not lifted up his soul unto vanity, nor sworn deceitfully" (verses 3-4). The choir sang "Ere Long the Vail Will Rend in Twain" (#29 in the newly printed hymnal compiled by Emma Smith), Sidney offered the invocation, the choir sang "O Happy Souls Who Pray" (#14), then Sidney preached a two-and-a-half-hour sermon based on Matthew 8:18–20, which includes: "The foxes have holes, and the birds of the air have nests; but the Son of man hath not where to lay his head" (verse 20).

Sidney conducted the sustaining of Joseph Smith as prophet and seer, first by quorums then by the entire congregation, who then sang "Now Let Us Rejoice," written by William W. Phelps. Following the intermission, the congregation sang "Adam-ondi-Ahman," another hymn by William, then Joseph preached, conducted a sustaining of general and local priesthood presidencies, and prophesied blessings upon the Saints for their sustaining vote. The congregation sang the hymn "How Pleasd and Blest Was I," then Joseph raised his hands in the air and read the dedicatory prayer which had been revealed to him the day before in his third floor temple office (see Doctrine and Covenants 109). In it he prayed, "And now we ask thee, Holy Father, in the name of Jesus Christ, the Son of thy bosom, . . . to accept of this house, the workmanship of the hand of us, thy servants, which thou didst command us to build" (Doctrine and Covenants 109:4). The congregation sang another hymn by William, "The Spirit of God," then Joseph conducted a sustaining of the dedicatory prayer.[143]

The sacrament was then blessed by Don Carlos Smith, Joseph's youngest brother and president of the high priests quorum. Joseph and Don Carlos

---

143 President Howard W. Hunter spoke of the Kirtland dedicatory prayer in the October 1994 General Conference. "Consider the majestic teachings in the great dedicatory prayer of the Kirtland Temple, a prayer the Prophet Joseph Smith said was given to him by revelation. It is a prayer that continues to be answered upon us individually, upon us as families, and upon us as a people because of the priesthood power the Lord has given us to use in His holy temples" (President Howard W. Hunter, "The Great Symbol of Our Membership," *Ensign*, October 1994, https://abn.churchofjesuschrist.org/study/ensign/1994/10/the-great-symbol-of-our-membership?lang=eng).

spoke, followed by Oliver Cowdery and Frederick G. Williams, who testified that an angel sat between him and Joseph Smith Sr. during the dedicatory prayer. Heber C. Kimball later spoke of this angel: "'He was a very tall personage, black eyes, white hair, and stoop shouldered; his garment was whole, extending to near his ankles; on his feet he had sandals. He was sent as a messenger to accept of the dedication.'"[144] Hyrum Smith and Sidney spoke, and they were followed by a conducting of the Hosanna Shout. Brigham Young spoke in tongues, David W. Patten interpreted, then Joseph pronounced a blessing upon the congregation, and the meeting was adjourned.

An Evening Meeting Following the Temple Dedication

After the Saints returned to their homes, the brethren holding the priesthood returned to the temple that evening, and the litany of spiritual manifestations picked up where they left off with the dedication service. David Whitmer "saw three angels passing up the south aisle." The Prophet recorded,

> George A. Smith arose and began to prophesy, when a noise was heard like the sound of a rushing mighty wind, which filled the Temple, and all the congregation simultaneously arose, being moved upon by an invisible power; many began to speak in tongues and prophesy; others saw glorious visions; and I beheld the Temple was filled with angels, which fact I declared to the congregation. The people of the neighborhood came running together (hearing an unusual sound within, and seeing a bright light like a pillar of fire resting upon the Temple), and were astonished at what was taking place.[145]

---

144 Orson F. Whitney, *Life of Heber C. Kimball, an Apostle: The Father and Founder of the British Mission* (Salt Lake City, Juvenile Instructor Office, 1888), 103.

145 Joseph Smith, *History of the Church of Jesus Christ of Latter-day Saints*, ed. B. H. Roberts (Salt Lake City: Deseret Book Company, 1948), 2:428.

View of the roof and top floor windows of the Kirtland Temple. Photo by Casey Paul Griffiths.

George himself added,

> "There were great manifestations of power, such as speaking in tongues, seeing visions, administration of angels. Many individuals bore testimony that they saw angels, and David Whitmer bore testimony that he saw three angels passing up the south aisle, and there came a shock on the house like the sound of a mighty rushing wind, and almost every man in the house arose, and hundreds of them were speaking in tongues, prophecying or declaring visions, almost with one voice."[146]

Oliver Cowdery added,

> "The Spirit was poured out—I saw the glory of God, like a great cloud, come down and rest upon the house, and fill the same like a mighty rushing wind. I also saw cloven tongues, like as of fire rest upon many, (for there were 316 present,) while they spake with other tongues and prophesied."[147]

---

146   Cowdery, Diary, 27 Mar. 1836, "Journal, 1835–1836," p. 185, fn 387 JSP.
147   Leonard J. Arrington, "Oliver Cowdery's Kirtland Ohio 'Sketch Book,'" *BYU Studies* 12, no. 4 (Summer 1972): 426.

Preparation for the Solemn Assembly

Window detail from the Kirtland Temple. Photo by Casey Paul Griffiths, courtesy Community of Christ.

In January 1833, the Lord taught the Saints how to conduct a solemn assembly, a meeting held separate from a temple dedication. "Tarry ye, tarry ye in this place, and call a solemn assembly even of those who are the first laborers in this last kingdom. . . . Therefore, verily I say unto you, my friends call your solemn assembly, as I have commanded you (Doctrine and Covenants 88:70, 117). On Tuesday, March 29, 1836, the First Presidency, Missouri Stake presidency, and the Kirtland and Missouri bishoprics gathered to prepare for the solemn assembly to be held the next day. The details are recorded in Joseph's history:

> At eleven o'clock, a. m., Presidents Joseph Smith, Jun., Frederick G. Williams, Sidney Rigdon, Hyrum Smith, and Oliver Cowdery, met in the most holy place in the Lord's House, and sought for a revelation from Him concerning the authorities of the Church going to Zion, and other important matters. After uniting in prayer, the voice of the Spirit was that we should come into this place three times, and also call the other presidents, the two Bishops and their counselors, each to stand in his place, and fast through the day and also the night, and that during this,

if we would humble ourselves, we should receive further communications from Him. After this word was received we immediately sent for the other brethren, who came.

The Presidency proceeded to ordain George Boosinger to the High Priesthood, and anoint him. This was in consequence of his having administered unto us in temporal things in our distress, and also because he left the place just previous to the dedication of the Lord's House, to bring us the temporal means, previously named. Soon after this, the word of the Lord came, through President Joseph Smith, Jun., that those who had entered the holy place, must not leave the house until morning, but send for such things as were necessary, and, also, during our stay, we must cleanse our feet and partake of the Sacrament that we might be made holy before Him, and thereby be qualified to officiate in our calling, upon the morrow, in washing the feet of the Elders

Accordingly, we proceeded to cleanse our faces and our feet, and then proceeded to wash one another's feet. President Sidney Rigdon first washed President Joseph Smith, Junior's feet, and then, in turn, was washed by him; after which President Rigdon washed President Joseph Smith, Sen., and Hyrum Smith. President Joseph Smith, Jun., washed President Frederick G. Williams, and then President Hyrum Smith washed President David Whitmer's and President Oliver Cowdery's feet. Then President David Whitmer washed President William W. Phelps' feet, and in turn President Phelps washed President John Whitmer's feet. The Bishops and their Counselors were then washed, after which we partook of the bread and wine. The Holy Spirit rested down upon us, and we continued in the Lord's House all night, prophesying and giving glory to God.[148]

---

148   Smith, *History of the Church*, 2:429–30.

The Solemn Assembly

Interior windows of the Kirtland Temple. Photo by Casey Paul Griffiths, courtesy Community of Christ.

In more recent times, the term *solemn assembly* is used in reference to the dedication of a temple. In 1836, the dedication meeting occurred three days before the solemn assembly was held. Joseph Smith recorded,

> At eight o'clock, according to appointment, the Presidency, the Twelve, the Seventies, the High Council, the Bishops and their entire quorums, the Elders and all the official members in this stake of Zion, amounting to about three hundred, met in the Temple of the Lord to attend to the ordinance of washing of feet. I ascended the pulpit, and remarked to the congregation that we had passed through many trials and afflictions since the organization of the Church, and that this is a year of jubilee to us, and a time of rejoicing, and that it was expedient for us to prepare bread and wine sufficient to make our hearts glad, as we should not, probably, leave this house until morning; to this end we should call on the brethren to make a contribution. The stewards passed round and took up a liberal contribution, and messengers were dispatched for bread and wine.
>
> Tubs, water, and towels were prepared, and I called the house to order, and the Presidency proceeded to wash the feet of the Twelve,

pronouncing many prophecies and blessings upon them in the name of the Lord Jesus; and then the Twelve proceeded to wash the feet of the Presidents of the several quorums. The brethren began to prophesy upon each other's heads, and upon the enemies of Christ, who inhabited Jackson county, Missouri; and continued prophesying, and blessing, and sealing them with hosanna and amen, until nearly seven o'clock in the evening.

The bread and the wine were then brought in, and I observed that we had fasted all the day, and lest we faint, as the Savior did so shall we do on this occasion; we shall bless the bread, and give it to the Twelve, and they to the multitude. While waiting, I made the following remarks: that the time that we were required to tarry in Kirtland to be endowed, would be fulfilled in a few days, and then the Elders would go forth, and each must stand for himself, as it was not necessary for them to be sent out, two by two, as in former times, but to go in all meekness, in sobriety, and preach Jesus Christ and Him crucified; not to contend with others on account of their faith, or systems of religion, but pursue a steady course.[149]

Harrison Burgess described his experience.

I was in a meeting for instruction in the upper part of the Temple, with about a hundred of the High Priests, Seventies and Elders. . . . I beheld the room lighted up with a peculiar light such as I had never seen before. It was soft and clear and the room looked to me as though it had neither roof nor floor to the building and I beheld the Prophet Joseph and Hyrum Smith and Roger Orton enveloped in the light: Joseph exclaimed aloud, "I behold the Savior, the Son of God." Hyrum said, "I behold the angels of heaven." Brother Orton exclaimed, "I behold the chariots of Israel." All who were in the room felt the power of God to that degree that many prophesied, and the power of God was made manifest, the remembrance of which will remain with me while I live upon the earth.[150]

The Prophet did not stay for the entire meeting but added important details in his history and compared the solemn assembly to the Day of Pentecost in the Book of Acts.

---

149   Smith, *History of the Church*, 2:430–31.
150   Harrison Burgess, "Sketch of a Well-Spent Life," in *Labors in the Vineyard*, Faith-Promoting Series 12 (Salt Lake City: Juvenile Instructor Office, 1884), 67.

I left the meeting in the charge of the Twelve, and retired about nine o'clock in the evening. The brethren continued exhorting, prophesying, and speaking in tongues until five o'clock in the morning. The Savior made His appearance to some, while angels ministered to others, and it was a Pentecost and an endowment indeed, long to be remembered, for the sound shall go forth from this place into all the world, and the occurrences of this day shall be handed down upon the pages of sacred history, to all generations; as the day of Pentecost, so shall this day be numbered and celebrated as a year of jubilee, and time of rejoicing to the Saints of the Most High God.[151]

A Second Dedication

View of the Kirtland Temple from the nearby cemetery. Photo by Casey Paul Griffiths.

When close to one thousand Saints could not be seated in the original temple dedication, Joseph Smith promised a second dedication service. On Thursday, March 31, Joseph delivered on his promise.

---

151   Smith, *History of the Church*, 2:432.

This day being set apart to perform again the ceremonies of the dedication for the benefit of those who could not get into the house on the preceding Sabbath, I repaired to the Temple at 8 a.m., in company with the Presidency, and arranged our door keepers and stewards as on the former occasion. We then opened the doors and a large congregation entered the house, and were comfortably seated. The authorities of the Church were seated, in their respective places, and the services of the day were commenced prosecuted, and terminated in the same manner as at the former dedication, and the Spirit of God rested upon the congregation, and great solemnity prevailed.[152]

William W. Phelps described this second dedication, indicating the attendees almost filled the meeting room, that it lasted until about 9 o'clock that night—five hours longer than first dedication—and that it surpassed the first "in sublimity, solemnity, order."[153]

---

152   Smith, *History of the Church*, 2:433.
153   William W. Phelps to Sally Phelps, April 1836, MS 810, L. Tom Perry Special
       Collections, Harold B. Library, Brigham Young University, Provo, Utah.

Doctrine and Covenants 110: The Savior Accepts the Temple and Keys Are Conferred

Central window on the backside of the Kirtland Temple. Just inside these windows is where Jesus Christ appeared to Joseph Smith and Oliver Cowdery. Photo by Casey Paul Griffiths.

A week following the dedication of the Temple, Joseph Smith and Oliver Cowdery receive a visit from the Lord himself. The heading to Doctrine and Covenants 110 includes a statement from the Prophet's history: "In the afternoon, I assisted the other Presidents in distributing the Lord's Supper to the Church, receiving it from the Twelve, whose privilege it was to officiate at the sacred desk this day. After having performed this service to my brethren, I retired to the pulpit, the veils being dropped, and bowed myself, with Oliver Cowdery, in solemn and silent prayer. After rising from prayer, the following vision was opened to both of us." The editors of The Joseph Smith Papers add a few details. They indicate the first veils, or curtains, dropped were the ones that separated the main floor into four sections. "According to Stephen Post, who participated in the day's meetings, the presidency then went to the pulpits for 'the confirmation & blessing of the children.' At some point during the meeting, more veils were lowered, enclosing the west pulpits and dividing them into their four levels. JS and Cowdery 'retired to the pulpit'—apparently the top tier, which was reserved for the presidency—where they bowed 'in solemn, but silent prayer to the Most High.'"[154]

Joseph recorded that he and Oliver "saw the Lord standing upon the breastwork of the pulpit, before us; and under his feet was a paved work of pure gold, in color like amber. His eyes were as a flame of fire; the hair of his head was white like the pure snow; his countenance shone above the brightness of the sun; and his voice was as the sound of the rushing of great waters" (Doctrine and Covenants 110:2–3). The Lord went on to tell them that their sins were forgiven them and that their hearts and the hearts of the Saints should rejoice, for he declared: "I have accepted this house, and my name shall be here; . . . the hearts of thousands and tens of thousands shall greatly rejoice in consequence of the blessings which shall be poured out, and the endowment with which my servants have been endowed in this house. And the fame of this house shall spread to foreign lands; and this is the beginning of the blessing which shall be poured out upon the heads of my people" (Doctrine and Covenants 110:7, 9–10).

When this vision closed, three heavenly messengers, at least two of whom had been translated at the end of their mortal experience, appeared and conferred priesthood keys upon Joseph and Oliver. First, Moses appeared and "committed unto [them] the keys of the gathering of Israel from the four parts of the earth, and the leading of the ten tribes from the land of the north" (verse 11). Oliver explained something of the reason for Moses's keys: "If the house is not built the Elders . . . can never go to the nations with the everlasting gospel."[155] Elder McConkie elaborated on Oliver's statement and compared the gathering in Moses's day to the gathering in our day.

> By the 3rd of April in 1836 many thousands had come out of the Egypt of the world into a promised land of gospel peace. And then the heavens were rent, the Great God sent Moses back to confer keys and powers upon mortals, and the way was prepared for the full gathering that would make the first flight out of Egypt seem as nothing. Since then, with increasing power and in great glory, we have gathered, from their Egyptian bondage as it were, the dispersed of Ephraim and a few others, initially to the mountains of America, but now into the stakes of Zion

---

154   "Historical Introduction," Visions, April 3, 1836 [D&C 110], JSP.
155   Oliver Cowdery to John F. Boynton, May 6, 1834, in Oliver Cowdery letterbook, Huntington Library, 45–46, as quoted in Prince, *Power from On High*, 32.

. . . When the ten tribes return they will come at the direction of the President of The Church. [156]

After Moses, "Elias appeared, and committed the dispensation of the gospel of Abraham, saying that in [them] and [their] seed all generations after [them] should be blessed" (verse 12). Elder McConkie explained we have limited knowledge of Elias's identity and the relationship between celestial marriage and the keys Elias conferred.

> We know not who he was in mortality. There were many prophets who bore that name and title. One was Noah. Apparently, this Elias lived in the day of Abraham, and may even have been Abraham himself. In any event he "committed the dispensation of the gospel of Abraham" (D&C 110:12)—not, be it noted, the gospel of Christ, for that had already been received, but the gospel of Abraham, meaning the great commission which God gave Abraham in his day. . . .
>
> . . . And so, the Lord be praised, the marriage discipline of Abraham was restored; it is the system that enables a family unit to continue in eternity; it is the system out of which eternal life grows.[157]

Following the visitation of Elias, "Elijah the prophet, who was taken to heaven without tasting death, stood before [them]" (verse 13) and conferred the keys of the sealing power. Of this, Elder McConkie also taught: "That these promises—made to Abraham, Isaac, and Jacob, and others of the fathers—might dwell in our hearts, (for we are the children of the prophets), Elijah came and conferred the sealing power upon his mortal fellow servants. By virtue of this sealing power all ordinances, both for the living and the dead, may be binding on earth and in heaven."[158]

Thus, the fulness of the priesthood received in the holy temple requires both sets of keys, the keys restored by both Elias and Elijah.

> When Elias came [in the Kirtland temple], he brought the gospel of Abraham, the divine commission that God gave Abraham, the marriage discipline that God gave Abraham. Elias restored celestial marriage, and

---

156 Bruce R. McConkie, "This Final Glorious Gospel Dispensation," *Ensign*, April 1980, https://abn.churchofjesuschrist.org/study/ensign/1980/04/this-final-glorious-gospel-dispensation?lang=eng.

157 McConkie, "This Final Glorious Gospel Dispensation."

158 McConkie, "This Final Glorious Gospel Dispensation."

Elijah came and brought the sealing power so the ordinance would be binding on earth and sealed in heaven; and it takes the ministry of both of them to accomplish the purposes of the Lord. Because they came, God has planted in my heart the promise made to the fathers. And so I go to the Salt Lake Temple and marry my wife for time and for all eternity, and so begins a new kingdom of God. And if we are faithful, that marriage exists here and it exists hereafter. And I have been given through that ordinance every promise that Abraham received. It is given on a conditional basis.[159]

A similar event occurred 1,800 years earlier. Peter, James, and John were taken to the Mount of Transfiguration six days after the Lord told Peter he would give him the keys of the kingdom. There the Lord was "transfigured before them: and his face did shine as the sun, and his raiment was white as the light. And, behold, there appeared unto them Moses and Elias talking with him" (Matthew 17:2–3). The Bible Dictionary indicates, "On the mount, the Savior, Moses, and Elias (Elijah; also John the Baptist) gave the promised keys of the priesthood to Peter, James, and John, which enabled these brethren to carry forth the work of the kingdom on the earth after the departure of Jesus. These keys were later given to all of the Twelve. [They] saw the Lord in a glorified and transfigured state, . . . a vision of the earth as it will appear in its future glorified condition; saw and conversed with Moses and Elijah, two translated beings; and heard the voice of the Father."

---

159   Bruce R. McConkie, "The Promises Made to the Fathers," in *Studies in Scripture Vol 3: Genesis to 2 Samuel*, ed. Kent P. Jackson and Robert L. Millet (Salt Lake City: Randall Book Co., 1985), 47–62.

Community Life at the Temple

Detail of the dedicatory plaque of the Kirtland Temple. Photo by Casey Paul Griffiths.

April 3, 1836, was by no means the last of the amazing spiritual manifestations given in the Kirtland Temple. Among other events, on April 5 and 6, during a priesthood meeting, there were more anointings, the washing of feet, the gift of tongues, a mighty wind, prophesying, and visions and angels. On May 1, during a meeting of Seventies and elders, visions and angels were seen again. As a pattern of temple usage unfolded, many more manifestations were had. In October 1836, a policy was established allowing other sects to use the temple when not used by the Saints. The papyrus and mummies associated with the Book of Abraham were stored in the temple beginning in November 1836. On December 1, 1836, the first patriarchal blessings were given by Joseph Smith Sr., the first patriarch of the Church, in the temple.

Worship services were held in the temple Sunday mornings, afternoons, and evenings. Choir practices were held other evenings and priesthood quorums met on weeknights on the third floor. The Kirtland High School also met on the third floor during the day, using a curriculum that extended from the "first principles of education" for young children to Hebrew for adults. Wilford Woodruff was a student there. Prayer meetings for all members were held Thursday evenings, and on the first Thursday of each month, fast and testimony meetings were held, lasting from 10 a.m. to 4 p.m.

Although testimony meetings officially began at 10 a.m., many Saints came early to pray privately. Once the meeting began, a short sermon was delivered, then the main floor veils of were lowered, dividing it into four compartments with men and women seated separately. Led by an elder, each small group spent the remainder of the day praying, bearing witness of the goodness of God, and recounting spiritual experiences. Spiritual gifts abounded: the sick were healed, prophesying was a regular occurrence along with speaking in tongues, and some beheld visions. At 3 p.m., the veils were raised, the four groups were combined into one, and the meeting continued for another hour. Prescindia Huntington described one such meeting:

> I was in the temple [at a fast meeting] with my sister Zina. The whole of the congregation were on their knees, praying vocally, for such was the custom at the close of these meetings when Father Smith presided; yet there was no confusion; the voices of the congregation mingled softly together. While the congregation was thus praying, we both heard, from one corner of the room above our heads, a choir of angels singing most beautifully. They were invisible to us, but myriads of angelic voices seemed to be united in singing some song of Zion, and their sweet harmony filled the temple of God. [160]

---

160   Tullidge, *Women of Mormondom*, 207.

The Temple After the Saints Departed

Many Saints carved their initials in the timbers of the Kirtland Temple. This is a possible carving by Martin Harris. Photograph by Casey Paul Griffiths, courtesy Community of Christ.

The body of the Saints mostly vacated Kirtland by the summer of 1838, although a few remained behind. Over the course of the four subsequent years, the population of Saints in Kirtland increased substantially until about 1842 when the First Presidency directed those in Kirtland to move to Nauvoo. Until that time, the Saints maintained control of the temple. A few Saints remained behind, but at this point, fourteen different groups who had broken off from the main body of the Church all claimed ownership and the right to use the temple. The final claim was made by The Reorganized Church of Jesus Christ of Latter Day Saints (now Community of Christ), who own and maintain the temple today.

Caretakers from Community of Christ have been excellent temple stewards, and all visitors owe them a debt of gratitude for how they have and continue to sacrifice to preserve this remarkable building. Indeed, the temple has become a symbol of unity and cooperation between our Church and theirs. Community of Christ allows our Church to use the temple for firesides, missionary trainings, an occasional sacrament meeting, priesthood meetings, and even video recording. In addition, members of our Church frequently provide service there in the form of gardening, cleaning, painting, and so forth, and the entrance fees paid by the thousands of visitors each year, ninety-five percent of whom are Latter-day Saints, contributes greatly to the cost of running and maintaining this wonderful edifice.

The Printing Office Next to the Temple

At the northwest corner of the temple stands a small plaque placed by the Community of Christ to mark the location of the Church printing office. The Lord had planned for the Saints to construct three temples in Kirtland, two in addition to the one that was actually built. One was to be "dedicated unto the Lord for the work of the presidency," and the other was "for the work of the printing of the translation of my scriptures, and all things whatsoever I shall command you" (Doctrine and Covenants 94:7, 8). He also said, "These two houses are not to be built until I give unto you a commandment concerning them" (verse 16). While the Saints waited for further direction from the Lord, they constructed a two-story building near the temple site in the spring of 1834. The building included an office for the First Presidency and a printing office on the second floor and a location for the School of the Prophets on the first floor. It was the place where the first Twelve Apostles and Presidents of the Quorums of Seventy in this dispensation were called, where the Lectures on Faith were delivered, where washings and anointings were performed, and where the second edition of the Book of Mormon and the first edition of the Doctrine and Covenants were printed.

Kirtland Cemetery

Kirtland cemetery is located just across the street from the temple. Photo by Casey Paul Griffiths.

Just across the street north of the temple, and directly south of Joseph Smith's home, sits the Kirtland Cemetery. Its significance in Church history stems from the notables whose remains are buried there, including Hyrum Smith's first wife, Jerusha, and a child they lost, Mary Smith. Also buried there are Thankful Pratt, Parley P. Pratt's first wife, John Johnson and two of his daughters, Emily and Mary, and Mary Duty Smith, Joseph Smith's grandmother. In the 1830s, a small Methodist meetinghouse stood on the cemetery lot's southeast corner.

Monument placed by the Smith family to honor the members of the family buried in Kirtland.
Photo by Acacia E. Griffiths.

Monument to Thankful Halsey Pratt, the first wife of Parley P. Pratt.
Photo by Acacia E. Griffiths.

Next to the Kirtland Temple, there is a small headstone, pockmarked with age, that reads simply "Oliver Granger." The stonemason who made the headstone failed to carefully carve the name and almost left the 'r' at the end of 'Granger' off the end of the monument. This simple marker designates the final resting place of Oliver Granger. In Doctrine and Covenants 117, Oliver Granger is called to "contend earnestly for the redemption of the First Presidency of my Church" (D&C 117:13). Joseph Smith later wrote in his history, "As I was driven away from Kirtland without the privilege of settling my business, I had previous to this employed Colonel Oliver Granger as my agent to close all my affairs in the Eastern States; and as I have been accused of 'running away, cheating my creditors'"[161] As the Church left Kirtland, Granger was asked to return and settle the debts of the Church in the area.

The headstone of Oliver Granger in the Kirtland Cemetery. Photo by Acacia E. Griffiths.

Granger served faithfully in this calling, laboring diligently to pay off debts and to answer accusations that the leaders of the Church had fled from Kirtland to avoid paying their debts. In appreciation for his willingness to fulfill this difficult task, the First Presidency wrote a letter of commendation to Granger in May 1839, which reads: "We have always found President Oliver Granger to be a man of the most strict integrity and moral virtue, and in

---

161   JS History, vol. B-1, p. 837, JSP.

fine to be a man of God. We have had long experience and acquaintance with Br Granger, we have entrusted vast business concerns to him which have been managed skillfully to the support of our Characters and interest, as well as that of the Church."[162] The letter also contains a blessing for Granger written in revelatory language, which declares, "And again Verily thus saith the Lord, I will lift up my servant Oliver, And beget for him a great name on the earth and among my people, because of the integrity of his soul; therefore let all my Saints abound unto him with all liberality and long suffering, and it shall be a blessing on their heads."[163]

Oliver Granger died in Kirtland under unknown conditions. But his name is still held "in sacred remembrance" (D&C 117:12) to this day for upholding the integrity of the Church and its leaders.

Stannard Rock Quarry

The Stannard Rock Quarry, where much of the stone for the Kirtland Temple was excavated.
Photo by Casey Paul Griffiths..

There were probably at least three different sandstone quarries from which stone for the temple was excavated, but the majority came from the Stannard

---

162   Authorization for Oliver Granger, 13 May 1839, pp. 45–46, JSP.
163   Authorization for Oliver Granger, 13 May 1839, p. 46, JSP.

Rock Quarry, which is located in Chapin Forest Reserve. Old drill marks can be seen along with regular score markings indicative of later excavations—most of the stone cut out for the temple was more rough cut and irregular.

Detail of an area of Stannard Rock Quarry where materials for the temple were gathered. Photo by Casey Paul Griffiths.

Stone excavation began with workmen hammering iron wedges into natural fissure lines or into drilled holes. They hammered each wedge in sequence multiple times until they forced the rock to split along the wedge line. The blocks of various sizes were shaped and trimmed with picks before being loaded onto wagons using a hand wench and pulley blocks with ropes. A blacksmith often set up a forge and worked alongside the workers in the quarry where he could make and sharpen tools for the stonecutters.

Saturdays were appointed for quarry work, and every available wagon and team was needed in order to keep the temple stone masons busy for a week. Workers reported to the quarry for many Saturdays; the temple walls were two-and-a-half feet thick and over sixty feet high. The Prophet sometimes worked as foreman in the quarries.

Mini-Devotional—A Pentecost and an Endowment

After the manifestations in the Kirtland Temple during its dedication, Joseph Smith recorded: "It was a Pentecost and endowment indeed, long to be remembered, for the sound shall go forth from this place into all the world, and the occurrences of this day shall be handed down upon the pages of sacred history to all generations; as the day of Pentecost."[164]

With you family, read over the marvelous manifestations that were given in the Kirtland Temple. Show pictures of the temple to highlight where these manifestations took place. Invite family members to visualize standing in the rooms as the manifestations were given. When you enter the temple, remind your family members of how they felt imagining what it would have been like to be present during those marvelous days when the Kirtland Temple was built and dedicated.

- What are some unique spiritual experiences you have had?
- Despite the Pentecostal experiences the Saints had in the Kirtland Temple, they fell into apostasy and the temple was abandoned less than two years after its dedication. Why do you think these spiritual outpourings failed to lead to lasting conversion for many of the Saints?
- What type of actions do you think lead to more lasting conversion?

---

164   Smith, *History of the Church*, 4: 432.

Significant events at this location:

- Inspired by the disciples in the New Testament, Isaac and Lucy Morley invited a number of believers to live with all things in common on their farm in Mentor, Ohio. Their actions partially inspired Joseph Smith to seek guidance about the best way to provide for the poor (see Doctrine and Covenants 42).

- In March 1831, Joseph and Emma Smith moved into a house on the Morley Farm. This served as their second home in the Kirtland area.

- On April 30, 1831, Emma Smith gave birth to twins. The twins died shortly after birth.

- On May 9, 1831, Joseph and Emma Smith adopted the twins of John and Julia Murdock, Julia having died in childbirth.

- In June 1831, a conference was held on the Morley Farm that featured the first ordinations to the office of high priest in this dispensation and led to a great spiritual outpouring.

- In the fall of 1831, Isaac and Lucy Morley sold their farm to purchase lands for the City of Zion.

- At a gathering in 1834 held in the schoolhouse on the Morley Farm, Joseph Smith prophesied that the Church would be establish throughout the world.

- Doctrine and Covenants 45, 46, 47, 48, 49, 50, 52, 53, 54, 55, 56, 63, and 64 were received while Joseph Smith was living on the Morley Farm.

THE ISAAC AND LUCY MORLEY FARM

The Historic Morley Farm. Photo by Kenneth Mays.

The Morley Farm was home to Joseph and Emma Smith for only six months in 1831, but during that time, many important events occurred. Joseph continued his inspired translation of the Bible and was commanded to begin translating the New Testament soon after moving to the Morley Farm. As the New York and Pennsylvania Saints gathered to Ohio, many settled on the Morley Farm. Most of the early Saints attempted to live the law of consecration and stewardship, which had been revealed earlier that year. Joseph and Emma lost their twins at birth but adopted the Murdock twins soon after. The fourth conference of the Church was held at the schoolhouse on the Morley Farm. During this conference, the first high priests were ordained, visions of deity were given, and the man of sin was revealed. Joseph also prophesied that "this Church will fill North and South America—it will fill the world" and that the Saints would go to the Rocky Mountains.[165]

Isaac and Lucy Morley and "the Family"

Photo of Isaac Morley, ca. 1850-65.
Courtesy International Society
Daughters of Utah Pioneers.

Isaac Morley was born in Montague, Massachusetts, on March 11, 1786, to Thomas E. Morley and Editha Marsh, who had nine children in all. His wife, Lucy Gunn, was also born in Montague that same year on January 24 to Asahel Gunn and Lucy Root, who had seven children.[166] Isaac's uncle Ezekiel was among those employed with Turhand Kirtland in 1797 to survey the part of the Western Reserve where Kirtland was eventually located. In 1811, Isaac traveled to the Kirtland area and acquired one hundred acres from Ezekiel on the "Kirtland Flats," a heavily wooded area that became the site of several industrial and merchandising enterprises and that was east of what became known as "Temple Hill." Isaac built a small cabin on the property and returned home to Salem in the fall to marry his childhood sweetheart, Lucy. They were married on June 20, 1812, and left for Ohio three days later. Lucy gave birth to at least nine children,[167] seven of whom survived to adulthood: Philena, Lucy Diantha, Aditha Ann, Calista, Cordelia, Theressa, and Isaac Jr.

The Morley family worked together to create a prosperous farm. They grew fruit trees, field crops, peppermint, and flax for linen cloth. Lucy constructed clothes for her family from the wool their herd of sheep provided. Isaac also worked as a cooper to make barrels he could sell and use in storing the maple syrup and honey he extracted from the trees and hives on their property. In

---

165   *Sixty-Eighth Annual Conference of the Church of Jesus Christ of Latter-day Saints* (Salt Lake City: Deseret News Publishing Company, 1898), 57.

166   "Lucy Morley (Gunn)," Geni, accessed August 31, 2022, https://www.geni.com/people/Lucy-Morley/6000000003682493400.

167   "Lucy Morley," Family Search, https://ancestors.familysearch.org/en/KWVM-MGT/lucy-gunn-1786-1848. The Geni.com reference lists fourteen children, two of whom are listed only as "Son Morley Twin" and "Daughter Morley Twin."

1814, they built a small, log cabin schoolhouse on a hilltop on the north side of their property. Here, the Morley children and the children of friends and neighbors received a basic education. They were also able to build and move into a frame house shortly thereafter.

In early 1828, the Morley family, along with other early settlers, joined with Sidney Rigdon in the Reformed Baptist movement. Possibly influenced by Robert Owen's promotion of communal living[168] or other nearby communal groups like the Shakers, Isaac was especially interested in the lifestyle of the ancient Saints to have "all things common" (Acts 2:44; 4:32). Following Sidney's direction in 1830, Isaac, his brother-in-law Titus Billings, and Lyman Wight influenced between fifty and one hundred people to join with them in a communal group called "the family" or "the big family." Most of "the family" built a string of cabins on the Morley farm and a few others gathered in Thompson, Ohio.

The Mission to the Lamanites and the Command to "Go to the Ohio"

Farmhouse at the Isaac and Lucy Morley Farm. Photo by Casey Paul Griffiths.

---

168 Frank Prodmore, *Robert Owen: A Biography* (New York: D. Appleton and Company, 1907).

On October 29, 1830, Parley P. Pratt, Oliver Cowdery, Peter Whitmer Jr., and Ziba Petersen arrived in Kirtland on their way to preach to the Lamanites. Because of Parley's association with Sidney Rigdon and his congregation, the four missionaries stopped in the Kirtland area to preach the restored gospel. Although their reception was intentionally met with skepticism, soon many began to see the truthfulness of the message and were baptized.[169] Isaac, Lucy, and four of the Morley children were baptized in November 1830. They were among the first Latter-day Saint converts and were joined by nearly all the adult members of "the family." The Morleys invited the missionaries to stay on the farm during their three-week stay in Kirtland. The Morley schoolhouse held many of the first Church meetings in Kirtland.

Before the missionaries left for western Missouri, they appointed Sidney as the leader of the Kirtland branch, one of the four branches of the Church they established in northeast Ohio. Isaac replaced him the following month when Sidney and Edward Partridge, who lived in nearby Painesville, traveled to New York to meet the Prophet (see Doctrine and Covenants 35–36). When the missionaries left Kirtland and continued their travels towards Missouri, there were 127 new converts to the faith.[170] After three months, the *Geauga Gazette*[171] reported that there were 200 converts in Kirtland village and at least 400 converts in the larger area.

With the arrival of Sydney and Edward to Fayette, New York, in December 1830, the Lord revealed that the Saints should "assemble together at the Ohio," (Doctrine and Covenants 37:3). In January 1831, the Lord promised: "Wherefore, for this cause I gave unto you the commandment that ye should go to the Ohio; and there I will give unto you my law; and there you shall be endowed with power from on high" (Doctrine and Covenants 38:32). Many of the Saints in New York and Pennsylvania gathered to Ohio beginning early in 1831. Joseph and Emma arrived around February 1.

When the Smiths arrived in Kirtland, Newel K. and Elizabeth Ann Whitney invited them stay in their home. Only a few days later, the Lord revealed to Joseph: "It is meet that my servant Joseph Smith, Jun., should have

---

169   *The Autobiography of Parley Parker Pratt, One of the Twelve Apostles of the Church of Jesus Christ of Latter-day Saints: Embracing His Life, Ministry and Travels, With Extracts, in Prose and Verse, From His Miscellaneous Writings,* ed. Parley P. Pratt (Chicago, IL: Law, King & Law, 1888), 50.

170   *Autobiography of Parley Parker Pratt,* 50.

171   "Fanaticism: The Golden Bible, or the Book of Mormon," *The Geauga Gazette,* February 1, 1831, http://www.sidneyrigdon.com/dbroadhu/OH/chrd1831.htm#020131.

a house built, in which to live and translate" (Doctrine and Covenants 41:7). A few weeks later, that commandment was fulfilled. The Morleys had a house built on their farm for the Smith family, and it was completed in the spring of 1831.

The Legacy of Isaac and Lucy Morley

Isaac and Lucy Morley remained converted to the Lord and his restored gospel throughout their lives. As part of the June 1831 conference, Isaac was ordained a high priest, one of the first receive that priesthood office. He was also among the first group of missionaries called to serve in western Missouri, and he served as a counselor to Bishop Edward Partridge at Kirtland and Independence, Missouri, where he also served as bishop. Isaac and Lucy were also affected by the mob attacks in Independence in 1833. He was one of the six brethren who offered their lives in exchange for relief of mob action against the Saints.[172] The men were jailed three nights and told they were to be executed the following day. Fortunately, they were able to escape.[173] The Morleys were among the Saints forced to flee Jackson County and escape into Clay County in November 1833. Isaac was appointed a member of the Missouri high council the following month. He then served a three-month mission to the eastern United States with Edward Partridge in 1835.

In 1836, the Morleys were forced into Caldwell County and experienced much of the Missouri persecutions. During this time, Isaac was ordained a patriarch and was also one of the brethren arrested and imprisoned for a time.

After the Morleys fled Missouri, they settled near Nauvoo where Isaac founded "Yelrome" (*Morley* spelled backwards) a settlement where most of Isaac's family lived, and where he served as bishop. He was later appointed as stake president at Lima, Illinois, then moved to Nauvoo in 1845 where he was admitted to the Council of Fifty. While in Nauvoo, Isaac was directed to enter into plural marriage. In 1844, he took Leonora Snow (the older sister of Lorenzo and Eliza R. Snow) as his second wife and Hannah Blakesley as his third, who bore an additional three children. Other wives were Hannah

---

172   Joseph Smith III and Heman Smith, *History of the Church of Jesus Christ of Latter-day Saints*, vol. 1, *1805–1835* (Lamoni, IA: Board of Publication of the Reorganized Church of Jesus Christ of Latter-day Saints, 1897), 316.

173   Hattie Esplin, *History of Isaac Morley.*

Knight Libby and Harriet Lucinda Cox, whom he married 1846, and Hannah Sibley and Nancy Anne Bache (also spelled as *Back*).

The Morleys left Nauvoo with many of the Saints in February 1846, and in early 1847, Lucy passed away while they were temporarily residing at Winter Quarters. After arriving in the Salt Lake Valley in 1848, Isaac was elected senator to the provisional state of Deseret in March 1849. Later that year, he was called to scout out the Sanpete Valley later that year, and eventually he was called to lead a group of Saints to the valley. Isaac presided over the area of Manti and eventually served as patriarch. His time in Sanpete was interrupted by a three-year return to the Salt Lake Valley as assigned by Brigham Young. He then moved to Santaquin (originally known as "Summit") in Utah County and finally to Fairview, Sanpete County. During this time in Utah, he served as member of the Utah territorial legislature for three terms. He died in Fairview, Sanpete County, in 1865 at the age of seventy-nine.

The Law of Consecration

This small teaching area at the Morley Farm is available for missionaries and families to use.
Photo by Casey Paul Griffiths.

Joseph and Emma Smith stayed in the home of Newel K. and Elizabeth Ann Whitney when they first arrived in Kirtland in February 1831. While there, the Prophet received the revelations that now constitute sections 41–44 in the Doctrine and Covenants. Some of these revelations include the earliest instructions for living the law of consecration and stewardship.

Those who lived on the Morley Farm, including "the family" and the recently relocated Saints from New York and Pennsylvania, continued to try and live the principle of all things common. However, when John Whitmer came to Kirtland in January 1831, his characterization of their communal efforts was not glowing: "The disciples had all things common and were going to destruction very fast as to temporal things: for they considered from reading the scripture that what belonged to a brother belonged to any of the brethren, therefore they would take each others clothes and other property and use it without leave: which brought on confusion and disappointments: for they did not understand the scripture."[174] After visiting "the family" on the Morley Farm, Levi Hancock recalled: "Hermon Bassett came to me and took my watch out of my pocket and walked off as though it was his. I thought he would bring it back soon but was disappointed as he sold it. I asked him what he meant by selling my watch. 'Oh, said he, I thought it was all in the family.' I told him I did not like such family doing and I would not bear it."[175] Other "family" problems included individuals moving between the Morley Farm and the other "family" established in nearby Chardon.

When Joseph and Emma arrived in Kirtland around February 1, 1831, they met the recent converts on the Morley Farm "to the joy and satisfaction of the saints."[176] It was in this context that the Lord revealed "the more perfect law of the Lord," or the law of consecration that comprised part of the revelation known in general terms as "the Law," now found in Doctrine and Covenants 42. When Joseph taught the law of consecration and stewardship to these recent converts, it resulted in the plan of "common stock" being "readily abandoned for the more perfect law of the Lord."[177] Although initially revealed during the month or so that Joseph lived in the Whitney home, much of the

---

174 John Whitmer, History, 1831–circa 1847, 11, The Joseph Smith Papers, accessed August 31, 2022, https://www.josephsmithpapers.org/paper-summary/john-whitmer-history-1831-circa-1847/15.

175 Levi Hancock, Autobiography, 1803–1836, 28, L. Tom Perry Special Collections, Harold B. Lee Library, Provo, Utah, accessed August 31, 2022, http://boap.org/LDS/Early-Saints/LHancock.html.

176 John Whitmer, History, 1831–circa 1847, 11, JSP.

177 Joseph Smith, *History of the Church of Jesus Christ of Latter-day Saints*, ed. B. H. Roberts (Salt Lake City: Deseret News, 1902), 1:146–47.

divine guidance that supported this law's implementation was received on the Morley Farm. "The Law" offered not only direction on how to "provide for [the] saints . . . in [God's] own way" (Doctrine and Covenants 104:15–16) but also a comprehensive economic order that provided for both spiritual and temporal salvation along with the means for financing the work of the kingdom.

Mini-Devotional – The Law of Consecration

The revelation Joseph received took the good intentions of people like Isaac and Lucy Morley and provided them with a structure designed to help and assist the poor. The Lord described the law of consecration as "a covenant and deed which cannot be broken" (Doctrine and Covenants 42:30). Since this time the Law of Consecration has served as one of the primary covenants the Lord asks members of the Church to enter into. In time, a commitment to live the Law of Consecration became one of the sacred covenants that Saints make in the temple. Take a minute to discuss or ponder the following:

- What are some ways that modern Latter-day Saints still live the Law of Consecration in our time?
- How can you seek to help others by living the principles of consecration?

Early Critics of the Church and Doctrine and Covenants 45

The School of the Prophets room in the Whitney Store. This small, unventilated room played a key role in the reception of the Word of Wisdom (Doctrine and Covenants 89). Photo by Acacia E. Griffiths.

Sometime around March 7, 1831,[178] while living on the Morley Farm, Joseph Smith received a revelation that was titled a "prophecy."[179] Joseph stated, "At this age of the church many false reports, lies, and fo[o]lish stories were published in the newspapers, and circulated in every direction, to prevent people from investigating the work, or embracing the faith."[180] With the baptism of 127 Saints in the Kirtland area,[181] and that number continually growing to some estimates of over 200 in Kirtland and more than 400 in the

---

178   John Whitmer copied the text into Revelation Book 1, where it is designated "A prophecy March 7th. 1831." Edward Partridge and William E. McLellin also made copies in 1831, but they assigned the date of March 6, 1831. The 1833 Book of Commandments dates this revelation to March 1831 and locates it at Kirtland, Ohio, while the 1835 Doctrine and Covenants specifies the date as March 7 but gives no location (Revelations Collection, Church History Library, Salt Lake City; William E. McLellin, Copies of Revelations, early November 1831, [1]–7, in "W. E. Mc.Lellan Jan—1877," 1877, William E. McLellin, Papers, 1831–1878, MS 13538, Church History Library, Salt Lake City; Book of Commandments 48, 1833, 103, JSP; Doctrine and Covenants 15, 1835, 128, JSP.

179   Revelation, circa March 7, 1831 [D&C 45], JSP.

180   Joseph Smith History, vol. A-1, 104, JSP.

181   *Autobiography of Parley Parker Pratt*, 48.

larger area,[182] many local newspapers began to take notice and write about the Church. Many of the articles were derogatory in nature and spread "false reports."

One of the strongest critics of the Church at that time was the editor and founder of the *Painesville Telegraph*, Eber D. Howe. In the November 16, 1830, issue, Eber included an article titled "The Golden Bible" and popularized the term *Mormonite*, becoming one of the first to use this term.[183] During the early days of the Church in Ohio, Eber's sisters, Widow Hutt and Harriet Hutt,[184] joined the Church, and sometime before April 1834, Eber's wife was baptized[185] and became a member of the Church he worked so passionately to discredit. In the *Painesville Telegraph*, Howe and those who wrote for him referred to members of the Church as "fanatics," "a gang of deluded mortals," "deluded beings," "dregs of this community," "profound believers in witchcraft, ghosts, goblins," and "inferior satellites."[186] They also called the Prophet's family a "gang of money diggers," and referred to the witnesses of the Book of Mormon as "pious reprobates."[187] Later in 1831, the *Telegraph* stated that Joseph's revelations were "volumes of . . . trash."[188] A misleading article in the *Telegraph* led Joseph to include the following in the *History of the Church*: "A great earth-quake in China, which destroyed from one to two hundred thousand inhabitants, was burlesqued in some papers, as 'Mormonism in China.'"[189] Eber's articles were circulated and reprinted in many newspapers throughout the country, all adding to Joseph's statement that many false stories were being "published in the newspapers, and circulated in every direction."[190] In 1834, Eber published *Mormonism Unvailed*, one of the first anti-Mormon books.

Another critic of the Church who was actively publishing disparaging articles in the spring of 1831 was Alexander Campbell. This was especially damaging in that many of the new converts of the budding Church in Ohio came from congregations that were originally formed as part of the Campbellite movement. Two of Alexander's in-laws were among the earliest converts to

---

182   Mark L. Staker, *Hearken, O Ye People: The Historical Setting of Joseph Smith's Ohio Revelations* (Salt Lake City: Greg Kofford Books, 2009), 71.

183   Staker, *Hearken, O Ye People*, 73.

184   Staker, *Hearken, O Ye People*, 72.

185   Joseph Smith, Journal, April 30, 1834, JSP.

186   Milton V. Backman, *The Heavens Resound: A History of the Latter-day Saints in Ohio 1830–1838*, (Salt Lake City: Deseret Book Company, 1983), 53.

187   Backman, *Heavens Resound*, 53–54.

188   Backman, *Heavens Resound*, 54.

189   Joseph Smith History, vol. A-1, 104, JSP.

190   Joseph Smith History, vol. A-1, 104, JSP.

the Church, Julia and John Murdock.[191] In addition to his Reformed Baptist movement, people felt Campbell's strong influence because of the two newspapers he founded, the *Christian Baptist* and *The Millennial Harbinger*. The first issue of *The Millennial Harbinger* was published on January 4, 1830 with the objective of "the destruction of Sectarianism, Infidelity, and Antichristian doctrine and practice. It shall have for its object the development, and introduction of that political and religious order of society called The Millennium, which will be the consummation of that ultimate amelioration of society proposed in the Christian Scriptures."[192] On February 5, 1831, Alexander published an article in *The Millennial Harbinger* titled "Delusions." It attacked the authenticity of the Book of Mormon. This article was published just months after the baptism of Sidney Rigdon and Parley P. Pratt, both of whom were preachers and leaders in the Campbellite movement in northeast Ohio. Of the Book of Mormon, Alexander stated that "every age of the world has produced impostors and delusions" and that the Book of Mormon was only "the most recent and the most impudent delusion which [had] appeared in [their] time."[193] This article was distributed throughout the country in various newspapers and became an early anti-Mormon tract.

It was articles written and distributed by Eber D. Howe, Alexander Campbell and others that led the Prophet to declare that many false and foolish reports were being circulated in papers. It was during this intense scrutiny that he petitioned the Lord on the matter. Joseph said, "But to the joy of the saints who had to struggle against everything that prejudice and wickedness could invent, I received the following."[194] Joseph received the "prophecy" that would later be known as section 45 of the Doctrine and Covenants.

Among other hopeful and inspiring doctrines, the "prophecy" addressed topics that would have been empowering to the Saints, especially in light of all the persecution they were suffering: New Jerusalem, Zion, gathering to safety, and the Second Coming of the Savior Jesus Christ. Through study of the Book

191   Staker, *Hearken, O Ye People*, 45.

192   Alexander Campbell, ed., *The Millennial Harbinger*, January 4, 1830, https://webfiles.acu.edu/departments/Library/HR/restmov_nov11/www.mun.ca/rels/restmov/texts/acampbell/tmh/MH0101.HTM.

193   Alexander Campbell, ed., "Delusions," *The Millennial Harbinger*, February 7, 1831, https://webfiles.acu.edu/departments/Library/HR/restmov_nov11/www.mun.ca/rels/restmov/texts/acampbell/tmh/MH0202.HTM#MH020208; Alexander Campbell, *Delusions: An Analysis of the Book of Mormon; with an Examination of Its Internal and External Evidences, and a Refutation of Its Pretences to Divine Authority* (Boston: Benjamin H. Greene, 1832), 5.

194   Joseph Smith History, vol. A-1, 104, JSP.

of Mormon and as he continued to translate the Bible, Joseph learned more about the City of Zion and the people of Enoch and the ushering in of the Second Coming of Jesus Christ and his kingdom. Learning more about Zion must have been an inspiring goal and a great comfort to the struggling Saints.

On February 9, 1831, shortly after the Prophet's arrival to Kirtland, the Lord instructed the Saints about what they needed to do while waiting for further revelation about Zion.[195] The Lord commanded, "Build up my church in every region—Until the time shall come when it shall be revealed unto you from on high, when the city of New Jerusalem shall be prepared, that ye may be gathered in one, that ye may be my people and I will be your God" (Doctrine and Covenants 42:8–9). Joseph was also told, "Thou shalt ask, and it shall be revealed unto you in mine own due time where the New Jerusalem shall be built" (verse 62).

Around March 7, 1831, Joseph received further clarification on the establishment of Zion. Against the backdrop of his Second Coming, the Lord instructed Joseph: "Ye hear of wars in foreign lands; but, behold, I say unto you, they are nigh, even at your doors" (Doctrine and Covenants 45:63). In helping the Saints better understand the need to move from their homes in New York and Pennsylvania and prepare them for future moves and sacrifices, the Lord taught

> Wherefore I, the Lord, have said, gather ye out from the eastern lands, assemble ye yourselves together ye elders of my church. . . . And with one heart and with one mind, gather up your riches that ye may purchase an inheritance which shall hereafter be appointed unto you. And it shall be called the New Jerusalem, a land of peace, a city of refuge, a place of safety for the saints of the Most High God; and the glory of the Lord shall be there, and the terror of the Lord also shall be there, insomuch that the wicked will not come unto it, and it shall be called Zion" (verses 64–67).

The Lord further instructed that "people must flee unto Zion for safety" (verse 68) and that Zion will "be the only people that shall not be at war one with another" (verse 69). The Lord also shared with the Saints this beautiful promise about Zion: "And it shall come to pass that the righteous shall be gathered out from among all nations, and shall come to Zion, singing with songs of everlasting joy" (verse 71). It is easy to see why Joseph stated that this revelation was a "joy of the Saints."[196]

---

195   Revelation, February 9, 1831 [D&C 42:1–72], p. [1], JSP.
196   Joseph Smith History, vol. A-1, 104, JSP.

Eventually, on June 6, 1831, Joseph received a revelation instructing him and many other elders to travel to Missouri. The Lord said that this land was "the land which [he would] consecrate unto [his] people" (Doctrine and Covenants 52: 2) and that if the Saints were faithful, they should "rejoice upon the land of Missouri, which is the land of [their] inheritance" (verse 42). Joseph left Kirtland on June 19 and arrived in Independence on July 14.[197] After arriving, Joseph began ruminating on the question of Zion. In his history, he stated, "When will the wilderness blossom as the rose; when will Zion be built up in her glory, and where will thy Temple stand unto which all nations shall come in the last days?"[198] On July 20, the Lord taught: "Missouri . . . is the land which I have appointed and consecrated for the gathering of the saints. Wherefore, this is the land of promise, and the place for the city of Zion. . . . Behold, the place which is now called Independence is the center place" (Doctrine and Covenants 57:1–3). Joseph and the Saints now knew that the City of Holiness, even Zion, was to be built in Independence, Missouri.

The Joseph Smith's Inspired Translation

In the "prophecy" revelation, the Lord also instructed Joseph Smith concerning his efforts in translating the Bible. Beginning in June 1830, Joseph and his scribes primarily focused on translating the Old Testament, beginning with the book of Genesis and the visions of Moses.[199] By April 5, 1831, Joseph and his scribes had created a sixty-one-page manuscript detailing the visions of Moses and a revised version of Genesis 1:1–24:41.[200] The Lord then instructed Joseph in this March 7 revelation to begin translating the New Testament so that he would "be prepared for the things to come" (Doctrine and Covenants 45:60–61). On March 8, 1831, Joseph with Sidney Rigdon as his scribe began translating the New Testament; they titled their document "A Translation of the New Testament translated by the power of God."[201] They began with Matthew 1:1 and translated sixty-five pages through Matthew 26:71 before their work was interrupted by their travels to Missouri in June 1831.[202]

---

197 William W. Phelps, "Extract of a Letter from the Late Editor," *Ontario Phoenix*, September 7, 1831, [2]; Joseph Smith History, vol. A-1, 126, JSP.
198 Joseph Smith History, vol. A-1, 127, JSP.
199 Old Testament Revision 1, p. [1], JSP.
200 Old Testament Revision 1, p. 61, JSP.
201 New Testament Revision 1, p. 1, JSP.
202 New Testament Revision 1, p. 63, JSP.

Religious Enthusiasm and
Doctrine and Covenants 46

The new coverts in Ohio had a difficult time reconciling previous religious traditions with their new faith. One of these traditions was the practice of "religious enthusiasm," or engaging in very dramatic and demonstrative behaviors supposedly inspired by the Holy Ghost. These demonstrations gave fodder to local critics like Eber D. Howe who portrayed rather graphic descriptions of religious enthusiasm among the Saints:

> Immediately after Mr. R[igdon] and the four pretended prophets left Kirtland, a scene of the wildest enthusiasm was exhibited, chiefly, however, among the young people; they would fall, as without strength, roll upon the floor, and, so mad were they that even the females were seen on a cold winter day, lying under the bare canopy of heaven, with no couch or pillow but the fleecy snow. At other times they exhibited all the apish actions imaginable, making grimaces both horrid and ridiculous, creeping upon their hands and feet, &c. Sometimes, in these exercises the young men would rise and play before the people, going through all the Indian maneuvers of knocking down, scalping, ripping open, and taking out the bowels. At other times, they would start and run several furlongs, then get upon stumps and preach to *imagined* congregations, baptize ghosts, &c. At other times, they are taken with a fit of jabbering after which they neither understood themselves nor anybody else, and this they call speaking foreign languages by divine inspiration. Again the young men are seen running over the hills in pursuit, they say, of balls of fire which they see flying through the air.[203]

John Whitmer took notice of the odd behaviors when he arrived in Kirtland, indicating that "the enemy of all righteous had got hold of some of those who professed to be his followers, because they had not sufficient knowledge to detect him in all his devices."[204] He went on to list what he observed in ways that aligned with Eber's depiction. "Some had visions and could not tell what they saw. Some would fancy to themselves that they had the sword of Laban, and would wield it as expert as a light dragoon, some would act like

---

203   Eber D. Howe, ed., "Mormonism," *Painesville Telegraph*, February 15, 1831, http://www.sidneyrigdon.com/dbroadhu/oh/paintel2.htm#021531.

204   John Whitmer, History, 1837-circa 1837, 10, JSP.

an Indian in the act of scalping, some would slide or scoot and [on] the floor, with the rapidity of a serpent, which the[y] termed sailing in the boat to the Lamanites, preaching the gospel. And many other vain and foolish manoeuvers that are unseeming, and unprofitable to mention. Thus the devil blinded the eyes of some good and honest disciples."[205]

In seeking answers to the problems of religious enthusiasm, Joseph Smith received a revelation (now found Doctrine and Covenants 46) that addressed the problem of false spiritual gifts, or religious enthusiasm. The Lord first indicated the source of these gifts as "evil spirits, or doctrine of devils, or the commandments of men" (verse 7). Adding a caution, "beware lest ye are deceived," the Lord indicated that the antidote was to "seek . . . earnestly the best gifts, always remembering for what they are given" (verse 8). In other words, the Saints should seek these gifts "for the benefit of those who love [God] and keep all [his] commandments, and him that seeketh so to do; . . . not for a sign that they may consume it upon their lusts" (verse 9). Then to clarify, the Lord provided a list of the gifts he gives to the Saints, "for there are many gifts and to every man is given a gift. . . . To some is given one, and to some is given another, that all may be profited thereby" (verses 11–12).

Armed with this revelation, the Prophet had at least some success in dealing with false spiritual manifestations. Around this time, Joseph wrote to his brother Hyrum: "I have been engaged in regulating the churches here as the disciples are numerous and the devil had made many attempts to overthrow them. It has been a serious job but the Lord is with us and we have overcome and have all things regular."[206]

"Let Us Reason Together": Doctrine and Covenants 50

The revelation found in Doctrine and Covenants 46 did not cause the Saints to cease practicing false religious enthusiasm. The list of gifts the Lord provided did not preclude other gifts, nor did he describe behaviors that were not legitimate spiritual manifestations, so there were disagreements among the Saints on those topics. In fact, John Corrill said that unusual behaviors being claimed as legitimate "rose to such a height that the elders became so dissatisfied with them that they determined to have something done about

205   John Whitmer, History, 1837-circa 1837, 26, JSP.
206   Joseph Smith to Hyrum Smith, March 3, 1831, JSP.

it."[207] Parley P. Pratt did not speak lightly when referring to the Saints' religious enthusiasm. He noted that upon his return from Missouri, these behaviors "grieved the servants of the Lord" and that "many would not turn from their folly, unless God would give a revelation." Parley suggested that their "weakness and inexperience" could result in errors in "judgment concerning these spiritual phenomena," causing he, John Murdock, and others to go "to Joseph Smith and ask . . . him to inquire of the Lord concerning these spirits or manifestations."[208] John Corrill called the resulting revelation, now found in Doctrine and Covenants 50, "very gratifying, for it condemned these visionary spirits, and gave rules for Judging of spirits in general."[209]

As Joseph introduced the revelation, the Lord stated he would address the issue of "the spirits which have gone abroad in the earth" (verse 1), including "false spirits, which have gone forth in the earth, deceiving the world" (verse 2). The Lord further revealed that Satan himself was involved in this attempt to "overthrow [the Saints]" (verse 3), and he characterized these false spiritual administrations as an "abomination in the church that profess [his] name" (verse 4). He acknowledged the presence of "deceivers and hypocrites" (verse 6) who had "given the adversary power" (verse 7), but he promised that they would ultimately be "detected . . . and cut off, either in life or death" (verse 8). He also promised that those influenced by the adversary would "be reclaimed" (verse 7).

The Lord called three elders[210] to "go forth among the churches [branches] and strengthen them by the word of exhortation" (verses 37-38), presumably addressing the problem of religious enthusiasm. Parley P. Pratt and John Corrill, who were instigators of the discussions leading to the revelation, were two of the three elders along with Joseph Wakefield. Edward Partridge apparently had not dealt adequately with the problem in his ecclesiastical position. The Lord declared, "In this thing my servant Edward Partridge is not justified" (verse 39). However, Edward was given a chance to "repent . . . and be forgiven" (verse 39), suggesting he would also bear some responsibility for correcting the problem. History records detail that the elders did utilize these revelations to regulate the Church in this matter for the next few months. The Prophet himself was also involved in correcting the problem when a few weeks later at

---

207   John Corrill, *A Brief History of the Church of Jesus Christ of Latter Day Saints*, 1839, 17, JSP.

208   *Autobiography of Parley Parker Pratt*, 61–62.

209   John Corrill, A Brief History of the Church of Jesus Christ of Latter Day Saints, 1839, 17, JSP.

210   "Elder" (topic entry), JSP.

a conference on the Morley farm, he discerned that manifestations shown to Harvey Whitlock and other brethren were of the devil. Likewise, Jared Carter recounted an experience in Amherst, Ohio. He and Sylvester Smith were attending to the sacrament when "a young woman [was] taken with an exercise that brought her on to the floor." Jared recalled, "We kneeled down and asked our Heavenly Father in the name of Christ that if that spirit that sister possessed was of him that he would give it to us, but we did not receive that spirit." Acting contrary to the revelation, Sylvester sought to cast out the spirit by laying his hands upon the sister but to no avail. After reviewing the revelation in section 50, apparently with a copy they had made for themselves which specifically directed the elders to "proclaim against the spirit," Jared "then arose and proclaimed against that spirit with a loud voice. . . . From that time forward that spirit never came in to the meeting when [he] was present."[211]

Mini-Devotional – "That Which is of God is Light"

In the revelation given to Joseph Smith, the Lord explained, "That which doth not edify is not of God, and is darkness. That which is of God is light; and he that receiveth light, and continueth in God, receiveth more light; and that light growth brighter and brighter until the perfect day" (Doctrine and Covenants 50:23-24). The Lord reasoned with the Saints that true communication from God edifies us and brings us more light. The word edify literally means "to build." Take a few moments to ponder or write about the following:

- What are some things in your life that are edifying increase their influence?
- What are some things that are not edifying and how decrease their influence?

---

211   Jared Carter, Journal, 1831–1833, 4–5, MS 1441, typescript, Church History Library, Salt Lake City.

Twins Born to Joseph and Emma Smith
and to John and Julia Murdock

John Murdock was born July 15, 1792, to Samuel Murdock and Eleanor Riggs. John was a man striving to find the truth of God in his life. He joined many religious sects but soon found that they left him uninterested, so he determined that "all the sects were out of the way."[212] Eventually he moved near Kirtland and tried to remain aloof from organized churches.

Julia Clapp was born February 23, 1796, to Orice Clapp and Phebe Blish in Middlefield, Massachusetts. Before the year 1820, the Clapp family moved to Mentor, Ohio. Not long after, John and Julia courted and then were married December 14, 1823, when John was thirty-one years old and Julia was twenty-seven. They had six children, including an infant that died at birth. The twins, Joseph S. and Julia, were born April 30, 1831 (some accounts state May 1, 1831).[213]

In the fall of 1830, John heard of missionaries visiting Kirtland and traveled to hear their message. In Kirtland, he received a Book of Mormon and stated: "The spirit of the Lord rested on me, witnessing to me of the truth of the work."[214] He also recalled, "About ten oclock [the next] morning, being Nov. 5th, 1830, I told the servants of the Lord that I was ready to walk with them into the water of baptism."[215] John was baptized on November 5, 1830, by Parley P. Pratt in the Chagrin River. His wife and other family members soon joined him in his newfound faith.

On April 30, 1831, after giving birth to the twins, Julia died. John stated, "My wife died . . . and left 5 living children. Two of them but six hours old."[216] Meanwhile Joseph and Emma Smith had recently moved into a newly built small frame home on the Morley Farm. On April 30, Emma prepared to give birth to twins but "had hard labor and the blood went to her head which

---

212   John Murdock, journal and autobiography, circa 1830–1867, 8, MS 1194, type-script, Church History Library, Salt Lake City.

213   John Murdock, journal and autobiography, circa 1830–1867, 7, MS 1194, type-script, Church History Library, Salt Lake City.

214   John Murdock, journal and autobiography, circa 1830–1867, 12, MS 1194, type-script, Church History Library, Salt Lake City.

215   John Murdock, journal and autobiography, circa 1830–1867, 12, MS 1194, type-script, Church History Library, Salt Lake City.

216   John Murdock, journal and autobiography, circa 1830–1867, 14, MS 1194, type-script, Church History Library, Salt Lake City.

became black." Joseph became frightened and called for the doctor who came and "bled her."[217] Both infants died within hours.

In his bereavement and needing to care for his two infant children, John Murdock placed his twins in the care of Emma and Joseph to raise and care for them. Emma would nurse and care for these twins throughout the summer of 1831. Unfortunately, Joseph S. did not live into adulthood. In March 1832, the twins were recovering from the measles while living at the Johnson family home in Hiram, Ohio. Joseph S. developed a cold after a mob forced the Prophet Joseph from their home and covered him in tar. Little Joseph S. never recovered and died on March 30, 1832. He was the fourth child Emma and Joseph lost in their first five years of marriage.[218] Julia, however, lived to be forty-nine years old. She was married twice but never had any children. She often found herself living with Emma in Nauvoo. Julia was with Emma when she died on April 30, 1879. Julia died of breast cancer on September 12, 1880 and is buried in Nauvoo, Illinois.

The June 1831 Conference

Pathway leading up to the site of the Morley Schoolhouse. Photo by Kenneth Mays.

---

217   Staker, *Hearken, O Ye People*, 309.
218   Joseph Smith History, vol. A-1, 209, JSP.

In the latter part of February 1831, the Lord directed "that the elders of [his] church should be called together" (Doctrine and Covenants 44:1) for a conference, a gathering for holders of the priesthood from their various missions and also for the general Church membership, and promised that if they were "faithful, and exercise[d] faith in [him], [he] will pour out [his] Spirit upon them in the day that they assemble themselves together" (verse 2). Early June was set as the time for the conference, the first to be held in Ohio, and letters and verbal notices were sent out to announce the dates. It was a four-day event: Friday, June 3 was a preparatory day, and the agenda for the conference was set by revelation;[219] Saturday, June 4 saw the Prophet introduce the office of high priest; Sunday, June 5 was a meeting for the general membership; and Monday, June 6 involved issuing mission calls following the commands in the revelation now found in Doctrine and Covenants 52.

As part of the preliminary instructions about the conference, the Lord revealed to Joseph: "Such of the elders as were considered worthy, should be ordained to the high priesthood,"[220] false spiritual gifts would be manifest as "the man of sin should be revealed,"[221] and some should see "their Savior, face to face."[222]

On June 4, 1831, sixty-three members of the priesthood, forty-four elders and nineteen priests and teachers, gathered in the small schoolhouse on the Morley Farm.[223] The conference session commenced with prayer and a long "exhortation" by the Prophet. Several brethren later wrote of its effect upon them. Jared Carter wrote that "not withstanding he is not naturally talented for a speaker yet he was filled with the power of the Holy Ghost so that he spoke as I never heard man speak for God, by the power of the Holy Ghost spoke in him."[224] Parley P. Pratt said that Joseph "spake in great power, as he was moved by the Holy Ghost; and the spirit of power and of testimony rested down upon the Elders in a marvelous manner."[225] Levi Hancock recalled that Joseph taught "the kingdom that Christ that he spoke of that was like a grain of mustard seed was now before him and some should see it put forth

219   "Historical Introduction," "Revelation, 6 June 1831 [D&C 52]," p. 89, JSP.

220   John Whitmer, History, 1831–circa 1847, 27, JSP.

221   John Whitmer, History, 1831–circa 1847, 28–29, JSP; see also 2 Thessalonians 2:3.

222   Ezra Booth, "Mormonism—No. IV," Ohio Star, November 3, 1831.

223   Minute Book 2, June 3, 1831, JSP; Levi Hancock, Autobiography, 1803–1836, 4, L. Tom Perry Special Collections, Harold B. Lee Library, Provo, Utah, accessed August 31, 2022, http://boap.org/LDS/Early-Saints/LHancock.html.

224   Jared Carter, Journal, 1831–1833, 4–5, MS 1441, typescript, Church History Library, Salt Lake City.

225   Autobiography of Parley Parker Pratt, 72.

its branches and the angels of heaven would some day come like birds to its branches just as the Saviour had said. Some of [them] shall live to see it come with great glory. Some of [them] must die for the testimony of this work."[226] John Whitmer added that "the Spirit of the Lord fell upon Joseph in an unusual manner" and that Joseph prophesied "that John the Revelator was then among the ten tribes of Israel . . . to prepare them for their return" and there were many other things spoken of in the conference.[227]

Joseph was followed by exhortation and prayer by Sidney Rigdon, and then all the elders present were invited to make exhortations. The minutes of the conference then record that Joseph ordained five brethren to the "high priesthood." Shortly thereafter, Lyman Wight ordained eighteen more, including Joseph himself. Later Bishop Edward Partridge "blessed those who were ordained in the name of Christ according to commandment."[228]

Prior to the ordinations, the Prophet had addressed Lyman Wight, saying: "You shall see the Lord and meet him near the corner of the house."[229] After his ordination, Lyman "stepped out on the floor and said, 'I now see God and Jesus Christ at his right hand let them kill me I should not feel death as I am now."[230] Joseph likewise testified, "'I now see God, and Jesus Christ at his right hand, let them kill me, I should not feel death as I am now.'"[231] John Whitmer added that Joseph "saw the heavens opened, and the Son of man sitting on the right hand of the Father, making intercession for his brethren, the Saints. He said that God would work a work in these last days that tongue cannot express, and the mind is not capable to conceive. The glory of the Lord shone around."[232]

---

226 Levi Hancock, Autobiography, 1803–1836, L. Tom Perry Special Collections, Harold B. Lee Library, Provo, Utah, accessed August 31, 2022, http://boap.org/LDS/Early-Saints/LHancock.html.

227 John Whitmer, History, 1831–circa 1847, 27, JSP.

228 "Generally, a divine mandate that church members were expected to obey; more specifically, a text dictated by JS in the first-person voice of Deity that served to communicate knowledge and instruction to JS and his followers" ("Commandment" [topic entry], JSP.

229 Levi Hancock, Autobiography, 1803–1836, L. Tom Perry Special Collections, Harold B. Lee Library, Provo, Utah, accessed August 31, 2022, http://boap.org/LDS/Early-Saints/LHancock.html.

230 *Autobiography of Parley Parker Pratt*, 72.

231 Levi Hancock, Autobiography, 1803–1836, L. Tom Perry Special Collections, Harold B. Lee Library, Provo, Utah, accessed August 31, 2022, http://boap.org/LDS/Early-Saints/LHancock.html.

232 John Whitmer, History, 1831–circa 1847, 28, JSP.

Other miraculous events accompanied the priesthood ordinations. Lyman Wight testified of "the visible manifestations of the power of God as plain as could have been on the day of Pentecost," including "the healing of the sick, casting out devils, speaking in unknown tongues, discerning of spirits, and prophesying with mighty power."[233]

In fulfillment of prophecy that the man of sin would be revealed, Harvey Whitlock was seized by a power following his ordination that caused bodily contortions and restricted his speech—common behaviors exhibited by the Saints who were engaging in false, ecstatic experiences. One observer stated that he turned black, his fingers were set like claws and his eyes were shaped like owls eyes—"a frightful object to the view of the beholder."[234] Joseph invited Harvey to speak, perhaps to test the source of the influences on him, but Harvey could only reply with signs. Hyrum Smith, Joseph's brother, expressed uneasiness: "Joseph, that is not of God."[235] After some discussion based on the principles of discernment given in section 50, Joseph rebuked the devil and cast him out. In that revelation, the Lord had said, "If you behold a spirit manifested that you cannot understand, and you receive not that spirit, ye shall ask of the Father in the name of Jesus; and if he give not unto you that spirit, then you may know that it is not of God. And it shall be given unto you, power over that spirit; and you shall proclaim against that spirit with a loud voice that it is not of God" (verses 31–32).

Of these events, John Corrill expressed: "The same visionary and marvellous spirits, spoken of before, got hold of some elders; it threw one from his seat to the floor; it bound another, so that for some time he could not use his limbs nor speak; and some other curious effects were experienced, but, by a mighty exertion, in the name of the Lord, it was exposed and shown to be from an evil source."[236] While the brethren were dealing with Levi Hancock's experience, ecstatic expression broke out amongst several brethren. Leman Copley, a 214-pound former Shaker "turned a complete summersault in the house and

233 Lyman Wight to Wilford Woodruff, August 24, 1857, Historian's Office, Histories of the Twelve, ca. 1858–1880, Church History Library, Salt Lake City.

234 Ezra Booth, "Mormonism—No. IV," *Ohio Star*, November 3, 1831.

235 Levi Hancock, Autobiography, 1803–1836, L. Tom Perry Special Collections, Harold B. Lee Library, Provo, Utah, accessed August 31, 2022, http://boap.org/LDS/Early-Saints/LHancock.html.

236 John Corrill, *A Brief History of the Church of Jesus Christ of Latter Day Saints*, 1839, 18, JSP.

came his back across a bench and lay helpless."[237] Joseph instructed Lyman to cast Satan out of Leman, which he did, but Satan "immediately entered another." Harvey Green fell "bound and screamed like a panther."[238] These terrifying experiences continued all day and well into the night, causing the leading brethren to deal with each on a one-to-one basis. It was understood that these experiences occurred "for the express purpose that the Elders should become acquainted with the devices of Satan; and after that they would possess knowledge sufficient to manage him."[239]

On Sunday, June 5, many Saints, including families, gathered on the Morley Farm to be taught by the Prophet. Levi Hancock said the Saints gathered "on the hill in a field where there was a large concourse of people collected."[240] In traveling to the conference, one woman fell from her wagon and "to every appearance was mortally bruised and she was not expected to live," but the next day, Simeon Carter "took her by the hand and said: 'I command you in the name of Jesus Christ to rise up and walk' and she arose and walked from room to room."[241] A number of long sermons were preached. Joseph preached one in which he said, "From that time on the elders would have large congregations to speak to and they must soon take their departure into the regions West."[242] Later that night, Joseph received a revelation. The next day he presented the revelation to the brethren assembled, calling many of them to travel as missionaries to western Missouri to hold a conference at which the Lord would reveal "the land of [their] inheritance" (Doctrine and Covenants 52:5). The revelations now found in Doctrine and Covenants 53–56 discuss the callings of missionaries to travel to Missouri. Joseph left with many of the missionaries on June 19, 1831 and returned to Kirtland on August 27, 1831.

237   Levi Hancock, Autobiography, 1803–1836, L. Tom Perry Special Collections, Harold B. Lee Library, Provo, Utah, accessed August 31, 2022, http://boap.org/LDS/Early-Saints/LHancock.html.

238   Levi Hancock, Autobiography, 1803–1836, L. Tom Perry Special Collections, Harold B. Lee Library, Provo, Utah, accessed August 31, 2022, http://boap.org/LDS/Early-Saints/LHancock.html.

239   Ezra Booth, "Mormonism—No. IV," *Ohio Star*, November 3, 1831.

240   Levi Hancock, Autobiography, 1803–1836, L. Tom Perry Special Collections, Harold B. Lee Library, Provo, Utah, accessed August 31, 2022, http://boap.org/LDS/Early-Saints/LHancock.html.

241   Jared Carter, Journal, 1831–1833, 4–5, MS 1441, typescript, Church History Library, Salt Lake City.

242   Levi Hancock, Autobiography, 1803–1836, L. Tom Perry Special Collections, Harold B. Lee Library, Provo, Utah, accessed August 31, 2022, http://boap.org/LDS/Early-Saints/LHancock.html.

A Vision of the Savior

In June 1831, Mary Elizabeth Rollins relates a remarkable experience that occurred the day of their arrival. She and her mother, who were among the early Kirtland converts, had walked to the Morley Farm to hear more about the Book of Mormon from the Prophet. When the Prophet saw the relatively large group, Mary recorded that he said: "'There are enough here to hold a little meeting.'"[243] Following prayer and singing, Mary indicated: "Joseph got up and began to speak to us. As he began to speak very solemnly and very earnestly all at once his countenance changed and he stood mute. Those who looked at him that day said there was a search light within him, over every part of his body."[244]

Shortly thereafter, the Prophet looked at the group and asked, "'Do you know who has been in your midst?'"[245] Joseph did not respond to the answer provided by one Smith family members: "'An angel of the Lord.'"[246] Martin Harris, who was sitting on a box at the Prophet's feet, said: "'It was our Lord and Savior, Jesus Christ.'"[247] Placing his hand on Martin, Joseph responded: "'God revealed that to you. Brothers and Sisters, the spirit of God has been in your midst. The Savior has been here this night and I want to tell you to remember it. There is a veil over your eyes for you could not endure to look upon Him. You must be fed with milk and not with strong meat. I want you to remember this as if it were the last thing that escaped my lips.'"[248]

Mary then described the effect of that experience and of what happened next. "These words are figured upon my brain and I never took my eye off his countenance. Then he knelt down and prayed. I have never heard anything like it before or since. I felt that he was talking to the Lord and that power rested upon us in every fiber of our bodies, and we received a sermon from the lips of the representative of God."[249]

---

243 Mary Elizabeth Lightner, "Remarks by Sister Mary E. Lightner Who Was Sealed to Joseph Smith in 1842," April 14, 1905, 1, typescript, Brigham Young University, Provo, Utah, https://contentdm.lib.byu.edu/digital/collection/p15999coll31/id/18292/.
244 Lightner, "Remarks," 1.
245 Lightner, "Remarks," 2.
246 Lightner, "Remarks," 2.
247 Lightner, "Remarks," 2.
248 Lightner, "Remarks," 2.
249 Lightner, "Remarks," 2.

Selling of the Morley Farm and
Doctrine and Covenants 63 and 64

Many of the elders who traveled to Missouri in June 1831 felt dejected by what they found and were very disappointed to learn that "the time has not yet come, for many years, for them to receive their inheritance in this land" (Doctrine and Covenants 58:44). They were then commanded to return to Ohio and raise money "to purchase lands in Zion" (Doctrine and Covenants 58:49). After a very tumultuous and faith-testing journey, many of the elders arrived back to Kirtland in late August and early September. Because of their disappointment and difficulties, some lost their faith in Joseph and fell away from the restored gospel, but Isaac Morley, after a period of testing, renewed his faith and made a tremendous sacrifice.

On August 30, 1831, the Lord reveled to Joseph: "My saints should be assembled upon the land of Zion," and those in "Kirtland [should] arrange their temporal concerns, who dwell upon this farm [the Morley Farm]" (Doctrine and Covenants 63:36, 38). He then commanded that Isaac Morley's brother-in-law Titus Billings "dispose of the land" and let the money "be sent up unto the land of Zion" (verses 39–40).

During the difficulties in Missouri, Isaac must have had moments of cynicism and doubt because the Lord chastised him, saying: "Behold, I, the Lord, was angry with him who was my servant Ezra Booth, and also my servant Isaac Morley, for they kept not the law, neither the commandment" (Doctrine and Covenants 64:15). But the Lord reassured Isaac, stating: "Nevertheless I have forgiven my servant Isaac Morley" (verse 16). He then advised that in order for Isaac to "not be tempted above which he is able to bear . . . his farm should be sold" (verse 20). Interestingly, the Lord then shared a glimpse of the timeline he had for the Saints in Kirtland, stating: "I, the Lord, will to retain a strong hold in the land of Kirtland, for the space of five years" (verse 21).

The Lord commanded the Morley Farm to be sold so that the Church could have money to purchase lands in Missouri. This meant that Joseph and Emma Smith could no longer live in their home that had been built on the property. By revelation, they were once again homeless. Knowing the Prophet's need for a home, John and Elsa Johnson invited Joseph and his family to live with them in their home in Hiram, Ohio. On September 12, 1831, the Smiths moved to the Johnson home. In October 1831, Titus Billings sold the Morley Farm, and Isaac and Lucy Morley took their family and traveled to Independence, Missouri.

"This Church Will Fill North and South America—It Will Fill the World"

Even after selling the Morley Farm in October 1831, the Church continued over the next few years to use the schoolhouse on the property for meetings and gatherings. One such gathering occurred on Sunday, April 27 1834, just four days before the first group of brethren would leave for Missouri with Zion's Camp and just one day after the arrival of Wilford Woodruff to Kirtland. Wilford recorded the following event:

On Sunday night the Prophet called on all who held the Priesthood to gather into the little log school house they had there. It was a small house, perhaps 14 feet square. But it held the whole of the Priesthood of the Church of Jesus Christ of Latter-day Saints who were then in the town of Kirtland, and who had gathered together to go off in Zion's camp. That was the first time I ever saw Oliver Cowdery, or heard him speak; the first time I ever saw Brigham Young and Heber C. Kimball, and the two Pratts, and Orson Hyde and many others. There were no Apostles in the Church then except Joseph Smith and Oliver Cowdery. When we got together the Prophet called upon the Elders of Israel with him to bear testimony of this work. Those that I have named spoke, and a good many that I have not named, bore their testimonies. When they got through the Prophet said, "Brethren I have been very much edified and instructed in your testimonies here tonight, but I want to say to you before the Lord, that you know no more concerning the destinies of this Church and kingdom than a babe upon its mother's lap. You don't comprehend it." I was rather surprised. He said "it is only a little handful of Priesthood you see here tonight, but this Church will fill North and South America—it will fill the world." Among other things he said, "it will fill the Rocky Mountains. There will be tens of thousands of Latter-day Saints who will be gathered in the Rocky Mountains, and there they will open the door for the establishing of the Gospel among the Lamanites, who will receive the Gospel and their endowments and the blessings of God. This people will go into the Rocky Mountains; they will there build temples to the Most High. They will raise up a posterity there, and the Latter-day Saints who dwell in these mountains will stand in the flesh until the coming of the Son of Man. The Son of Man will come to them while in the Rocky Mountains."[250]

250 *Sixty-Eighth Annual Conference of the Church of Jesus Christ of Latter-day Saints* (Salt Lake City: Deseret News Publishing Company, 1898), 57.

Significant events at this location:

- In September 1831, Joseph and Emma Smith with their newly adopted twins, Joseph and Julia, moved to the John and Elsa Johnson Farm in Hiram, Ohio.

- On November 1, 1831, a conference held in the Johnson home determined to publish the revelations of Joseph Smith as a new volume of scripture, which eventually became the Doctrine and Covenants.

- On February 16, 1832, Joseph Smith and Sidney Rigdon saw a vision of the Father and the Son along with a vision "concerning the church of the first born and the economy of God and his vast creation throughout all eternity."[251]

- On March 25, 1832, Joseph and Sidney were violently attacked by a mob.

- Sometime in the summer of 1832, it is likely that Joseph wrote down the earliest account of the First Vision while staying in the Johnson home.

- Doctrine and Covenants 1, 65, 66, 67, 68, 69, 70, 71, 73, 76, 77, 79, 80, 81, 99, and 133 were received at the Johnson Farm.

---

251 Vision, February 16, 1832 [D&C 76], 1, JSP.

The John and Elsa Johnson Home

Joseph and Emma Smith lived in the home of John and Elsa Johnson from 1832-1833. Photo by Casey Paul Griffiths.

In a revelation given September 11, 1831, the Lord commanded the Morley Farm to be sold and the money earned to be used to buy property in Missouri. Since Joseph and Emma Smith, along with their adopted twins, Joseph and Julia, were living in a house on the Morley Farm, they needed find a new place to stay. Without hesitation, John and Elsa Johnson invited the Smith family to move in with them in their large Vermont-style home in Hiram, Ohio. The little family moved in on September 12, 1832, and moved out exactly one year later. The time Joseph and Emma lived in the Johnson home was a period of divine guidance and direction. During the year they stayed at the Johnson Farm, Joseph received sixteen sections of the Doctrine and Covenants, received five additional revelations, and completed about half of the inspired translation of the Bible. Joseph and Emma would also experience great trials with the events surrounding Joseph being tarred by a mob and the death their child Joseph.

The restored Johnson home was dedicated on October 28, 2001. During the service, President Gordon B. Hinckley referred to the home as "'a place which will have the mark of immortality in the history of this people.'" He expounded, "'So long as this Church lasts, so long as it goes across the earth, so long as its history is written and known, the John Johnson home will have a prominent place in that history. . . . The power of God that was expressed here and known here . . . has gone over the earth, and we have scarcely seen the beginning of it, my brothers and sisters. . . . It will go forward, and whereas there are 11 million [Church members] now, there will be uncounted millions.'"[252] In his dedicatory prayer, President Hinckley continued:

> "We dedicate and consecrate the John Johnson home as a place sacred unto Thee and unto us, as a place in which Thou didst reveal Thyself with Thy Beloved Son, as a place in which the Prophet lived and translated the Bible, as well as brought forth under the direction of Thy Son many revelations, and as a place where he suffered so terribly. . . .
>
> "May this home continue now as a reminder to our people from far and near who may come to visit us, that Thou dost live; that Thou dost speak; that Thy Son lives and dost speak; and that a Prophet has recorded the things which Thou hast spoken on these premises and held them sacred unto us who live in this favored time."[253]

Because of the events that transpired in the year the Prophet and his family lived in Hiram, Ohio—including the doctrines and revelations that were restored to the earth—the Johnson home has become a sacred and historically significant location as well as a destination for many who seek to better understand the history of The Church of Jesus Christ of Latter-day Saints and the many early Saints who helped shape its foundation.

John and Elsa Johnson's Early Lives

John Johnson was born on April 11, 1778, to Israel Johnson and Abigail Higgins. He was raised in Chesterfield, New Hampshire, on the Connecticut

---

252   "President Hinckley Dedicates John Johnson Home," *Ensign*, January 2002.
253   "President Hinckley Dedicates John Johnson Home."

River. As a young man, John moved across the Connecticut River to nearby Dummerston, Vermont, with several of his brothers, looking for work. There he apprenticed as a cabinetmaker and purchased land.

Alice Jacob, usually known as Elsa, was born in Dighton, Massachusetts, on April 17, 1781, to Joseph Jacob (occasionally spelled Jacobs) and Hannah Beal. Around age ten, she moved with her family to Putney, Vermont, which adjoins Dummerston, where she eventually met John.

In compliance with local law for civil marriage, John and Elsa gave public notice of their intentions in Febuary 1800[254] and were married June 22, 1800. Following the birth of their first child, Alice, they moved to Pomfret, Vermont, where they had purchased eighty-two acres. John built a substantial farm, and Elsa gave birth to five boys and three girls, seven of whom survived to adulthood.

A Volcano and an Exodus

The largest volcanic explosion in the last 10,000 years of recorded history[255] occurred in 1815 when Mt. Tambora on the island of Sumbawa, Indonesia, erupted. The volcano discharged over 150 cubic kilometers of ash and gas into the air, which was carried by prevailing winds around the earth. This massive pollution absorbed and reflected sunlight, lowering the earth's temperature and causing dramatic weather changes all the way from China, across Asia, into Europe, and even into the northeastern United States. The year 1816 was referred to as "the year without a summer."[256] Frost occurred every month in that year, several inches of snow fell in June, and ice formed on ponds, resulting in widespread crop failure and severe financial hardships for those whose livelihood depended on agriculture. Thousands of farmers were forced to move west to find new land. Among these were the family of Joseph and Lucy Mack Smith, who moved to western New York in 1816, and the family of John and Elsa Johnson, who moved to Ohio's Western Reserve in 1818. The Johnsons

---

254 Putney, Windham County, Vermont Town Records, 1796–1833, in Mark L. Staker, *Hearken, O Ye People: The Historical Setting of Joseph Smith's Ohio Revelations* (Salt Lake City: Greg Kofford Books, 2009), 451.

255 Robert Evans, "Blast from the Past," *Smithsonian Magazine*, July 2002.

256 William K. Klingaman and Nicholas P. Klingaman, *The Year Without Summer* (New York: Saint Martin's Press, LLC, 2002).

were undoubtedly influenced by New England newspapers that had advertised land in the Western Reserve as inexpensive and quite suitable for agriculture.[257]

The Johnsons, accompanied by three of Elsa's sisters and their families and two other couples, left for Ohio on January23, 1818. Winter travel was cold, and the children later recalled deep snow, but frozen roads enabled travel by sled or sleigh with the potential to arrive in time for spring planting. They arrived in Hiram Township in Portage County on March 4, after a trip of six weeks. Elsa, who was seven months pregnant at the time, gave birth to her tenth child, Mary, in May. She gave birth to four more children while in Hiram, but only two of them survived. So many immigrants from Vermont settled in Hiram that it became known as "Vermont Colony."[258]

Within two weeks of their arrival to Hiram, John purchased an existing one-hundred-acre farm on "Pioneer Trail," the main thoroughfare joining the cities of Nelson, Hiram, and Mantua in Ohio. Some of the farm was already under cultivation, and it had several buildings, including a log cabin where the Johnsons would live while they continued to improve their farm and eventually build a more suitable frame home.

Dairy Farm, Products, and Home

Equipment and Storage building at the John and Elsa Johnson Farm. Photo by Acacia E. Griffiths.

257   L. D. Stilwell, *Migration from Vermont* (Vermont Historical Society), in Staker, *Hearken, O Ye People.*

258   Amos Sutton Hayden, *Early History of the Disciples in the Western Reserve, Ohio* (Cincinnati, OH: Chase and Hall, 1875), 246.

The Johnsons had the best dairy facilities and the second largest dairy herd in the Hiram area (they owned ten to twenty cows), and they shipped the cheese and butter they produced down the Cuyahoga River to southern markets and eventually eastward via the Ohio and Erie Canal.[259] The Johnson boys milked the cows twice a day, and Elsa worked with her daughters churning butter and making cheese. To make cheese, they cooked milk in large iron kettles, stirring the stiff curd constantly. They then poured it into cheese presses, tightened the presses, and eventually laid the cheese rounds to cool.

With the Johnsons' hard work and frugality, along with John's business acumen, they became one of the most financially prosperous families in Portage County, if not in the entire state.[260] They were able to enlarge the farm twice—by sixty then by eight acres—and to purchase a second one-hundred-acre farm that they later sold to John Jr. The Johnsons used their profits first to help extended family members immigrate and then to hire contractors to build a three-story, nearly four-thousand-square-foot home (attic included) for their family in 1828.[261] This new home included both a regular and a summer kitchen, two parlors, a large pantry, two bedrooms, and a carriage house— all on the main floor. The upstairs consisted of three bedrooms, one of which was later divided into two, a workroom for spinning and making fabric, and a large attic space above the summer kitchen and the carriage house, later used to accommodate many of the visitors who assisted the Prophet. There was also a cellar with a foundation, which provided a place where cheese rounds were turned daily and rubbed down with brine. Since the cellar was underground, the temperature could be adjusted for cheese production by opening and closing several windows or by burning a fire in the chimney, which originated in the cellar and extended up through the two upper floors and the attic.

259   Michael Rotman, "Ohio and Erie Canal: Building a Connection Between Lake Erie and the Ohio River," Cleveland Historical, https://clevelandhistorical.org/items/show/52.

260   *Johnson Home Historic Guide*, Church History Department (Salt Lake City: The Church of Jesus Christ of Latter-day Saints, 2009), 15.

261   There is some question as to when the Johnsons built and moved into their new frame home. Staker, *Hearken, O Ye People*, 281, indicates they were moved in by 1826. Other sources suggest 1828 (see, e.g., *Johnson Home Historic Guide*, 15; Michael R. Caldwell, *The John Johnson Family of Hiram, Ohio: "For He is a Descendant of Joseph,"* [Denver, CO: Outskirts Press, 2016], 19).

Friends, Religion, and Conversion

Tours at the John and Elsa Johnson Home start where the stables were once located. Photo by Acacia E. Griffiths.

At the time the Johnson family settled in Hiram, two religious denominations prevailed in the area—Baptists and Methodists. Some Baptists, including the Oliver and Rosetta Snow family[262] and other future Latter-day Saints, followed the restorationist teachings of Sidney Rigdon. The Methodists, led by the cultured and eloquent Ezra Booth,[263] counted the Johnsons among their earliest converts in 1826. Their neighbors and good friends immediately to the east, Symonds and Mehitable Ryder,[264] who had arrived in Ohio in 1814, were Rigdonite pillars.[265] Symonds's younger brother, Jason, who owned the farm adjacent to the Johnsons, married Fanny Johnson, a union that strengthened Johnson-Ryder relations.

---

262   John J. Hammond, *The Quest for the New Jerusalem: A Mormon Generational Saga* (Bloomington, IN: XLibris Corporation, 2012), 3:15.

263   Elliot I. Osgood, *Centennial History of the Hiram Church 1835–1935* (Hiram, OH: Hiram Historical Society, 1935), 5.

264   Hayden, *History of the Disciples*, 221

265   Francis Marion Green, *Hiram College and Western Reserve Eclectic Institute* (Cleveland: O.S. Hubbell Printing Company, 1901), 352.

In February 1831, on a trip to Kirtland, nineteen-year-old Lyman Johnson met Sidney Rigdon, who taught him the restored gospel and soon baptized him. Returning home, Lyman announced to his parents that he had joined the "Mormonites,"[266] causing them to be somewhat concerned. They counseled with their religious leader, Ezra Booth, who obtained a copy of the Book of Mormon, and accompanied by his wife, Dorcas, took it to the Johnsons' home. As Marinda Johnson later described, the Booths and John and Elsa "sat up all night reading it, and were very much exercised over it."[267] By the following morning, all four of them had experienced the spirit and power of the Book of Mormon. As Ezra later wrote, "The impressions of my mind were deep and powerful, and my feelings were excited to a degree to which I had been a stranger. Like a ghost, it haunted me by night and by day."[268]

Following this experience, the four traveled to meet the Prophet Joseph Smith in Kirtland. They were accompanied by Symonds Ryder and a Dr. Wright of nearby Wyndham. During a small gathering of members in the Whitney home parlor, the topic of spiritual gifts was discussed, prompting Elsa to ask the Prophet if the power to heal had been restored. She had been afflicted for two years with "chronic rheumatism in the shoulder,"[269] and her right arm had been virtually useless. He replied that healing had been restored, but he waited until the next day for the ideal time and place to lay his hands upon Elsa and pronounce a healing blessing by the authority of the priesthood. Elsa's right arm was instantly restored, as strong and useful as her left.[270]

The two couples were baptized shortly after Elsa's healing, and they returned to Hiram. Joseph and Sidney soon followed them and began preaching there. Word of Elsa's healing spread, influencing many to attend crowded preaching sessions. As many as twenty converts at a time[271] were baptized in a creek west of the Johnson home. Those converts eventually included all of the Johnson children except Olmstead, who chose not to associate with the Church. Other missionaries followed in the wake of the Prophet and Sidney,

266 Eber D. Howe, *Mormonism Unvailed* (Painesville, OH, 1834), 216.

267 Edward W. Tullidge, ed., *The Women of Mormondom* (New York: Tullidge & Crandall, 1877), 403.

268 Howe, *Mormonism Unvailed*, 176.

269 Luke Johnson, "History of Luke Johnson," *The Latter-day Saints' Millennial Star*, December 31, 1864, 834.

270 Philo Dibble, "Philo Dibble's Narrative," *Early Scenes in Church History*, Faith-Promoting Series 8 (Salt Lake City: Juvenile Instructor Office, 1882; Salt Lake City: Bookcraft, 1968), 79.

271 *Johnson Home Historic Guide*, 18.

and branches were soon formed in Hiram and nearby Nelson.[272] By the time the Smiths moved to Hiram on September 12, possibly as many as one hundred had been converted in the area surrounding Hiram.[273]

A Home for the Smiths with the Johnsons

Joseph and Emma Smith made their home with the Johnson family during the winter of 1831-1832. During part of the time they slept in this bedroom. Photo by Casey Paul Griffiths.

On February 4, 1831, the Lord commanded that Joseph and Emma Smith receive their own home: "And again, it is meet that my servant Joseph Smith, Jun., should have a house built, in which to live and translate" (Doctrine and Covenants 41:7).

Sometime in March, before Elsa's healing, Joseph and Emma had moved into a house on Isaac and Lucy Morley's farm about a mile east of the Whitney's home in Kirtland.

In a revelation in September 1831, the Lord told Isaac Morley "that his farm should be sold" (Doctrine and Covenants 64:20). This direction meant that eventually all the Saints living there, including the Prophet's family,

---

272   John Whitmer, History, 1831–circa 1847, 24, JSP.
273   Levi Jackman, "A Short Sketch of the Life of Levi Jackman," ca. 1851, M270.1
      J123ja 18--?, typescript, Church History Library, Salt Lake City.

would be required to move, so the Johnsons invited the Smith family to live with them.[274] Joseph, Emma, Julia, and little Joseph Smith moved to Hiram on September 12, 1831. At the same time, Sidney and Phoebe Rigdon and their family of six children moved into the log cabin across the Pioneer Trail from the Johnson home. Hiram provided a peaceful location where Joseph and Sidney could focus on the inspired translation of Bible. Much of the translation took place in the Johnson home.

When the Smiths moved in, only two of the Johnson children still lived at home—Mary and Justin. Alice, Fanny, and John Jr. had married and established their own households. Olmstead was away pursuing his own occupational "adventures," Luke and Lyman were often away on missions, and Emily and Marinda were at boarding school. The Lord had directed the Saints to provide assistance to the Prophet's family so the inspired translation could progress unhindered, and the Johnsons assumed much of that responsibility. The Johnson home proved to be a location where Joseph received much revelation.

Doctrine and Covenants 66: William McLellin

Photo of William McLellin, ca. 1865.
Courtesy Joseph Smith Papers.

On October 29, 1831, shortly after Joseph Smith and his family moved to the Johnson home, Joseph received a revelation on behalf of William E. McLellin. William had prayed in secret requesting for answers to specific questions, which he used to test whether Joseph was truly a prophet of God. William served as recorder of the revelation when it was given.[275] William first heard the gospel in Paris, Illinois, where David Whitmer and Harvey Whitlock were conducting an outdoor meeting enroute to Jackson County, Missouri (see Doctrine and Covenants 52:25). Desiring to meet the Prophet, William traveled to Jackson

274   Dibble, "Philo Dibble's Narrative," 79.
275   "Historical Introduction," Revelation, October 29, 1831 [D&C 66], The Joseph Smith Papers, JSP.

County, Missouri, but by the time he arrived, Joseph had already returned to Kirtland. Though disappointed, he listened to Hyrum Smith in a private, four-hour discussion on August 19, 1831. The following day, he recorded in his journal: "I rose early and betook myself in earnest prayer to God to direct me into truth, and from all the light that I could gain by examinations, searches, and researches, I was bound as an honest man to acknowledge the truths and validity of the Book of Mormon and also that I had found the people of the Lord—the living Church of Christ. Consequently, as soon as we took breakfast I told Elder Smith that I wanted him to baptize me . . . and [was] baptized the next day."[276]

In late October, William traveled to Orange, Ohio, to attend a conference at which he "first saw brother Joseph the Seer" and was ordained a high priest by Oliver Cowdery. He added, "This conference was attended by me with much spiritual edification & comfort to my heart."[277] Following the conference, William received another manifestation of the Prophet's divine calling while journeying to Kirtland: "I stepped off of a large log and strained my ankle very badly. . . . [Joseph] laid his hands on [the ankle] . . . and it was healed although It was swelled much and had pained me severely."[278] Despite these experiences, William showed an inclination toward sign seeking when he chose to test the authenticity of Joseph's calling. He wrote that he "went before the Lord in secret, and on my knees asked him to reveal the answer to five questions through his Prophet."[279]

Then on October, 29, 1831, without informing Joseph of his secret prayer and five questions, William asked Joseph to seek for divine guidance on his behalf. In response to this request, Joseph received a revelation, now found in Doctrine and Covenants 66. The Lord's response included answers to William's five questions, although the historical record does not specify their substance. Even after these miraculous experiences, William would later leave the Church and abandon his call to serve. In 1848, after being out of the Church for ten years, William still regarded this revelation as a witness of the Prophet's divine calling: "I now testify in the fear of God that every question which I had thus lodged in the ears of the Lord of Sabbaoth, were answered to my full and

---

276   Jan Shipps and John W. Welch, eds., *The Journals of William E. McLellin, 1831–1836* (Provo, UT: BYU Studies; Urbana: University of Illinois Press, 1994), 49.

277   Shipps and Welch, *Journals of William E. McLellin*, 33.

278   Shipps and Welch, *Journals of William E. McLellin*, 44–45.

279   Shipps and Welch, *Journals of William E. McLellin*, 45.

entire satisfaction. I desired it for a testimony of Joseph's inspiration. And I to this day consider it to me an evidence a witness which I cannot refute."[280]

Doctrine and Covenants 65: Missionary Work

On Sunday, October 30, 1831, the day following the revelation dictated to William McLellin, a congregation gathered at the Johnson home to worship. During the meeting, William spoke for an hour and a half, later recalling: "And it was not I but the spirit and power of God which was in me."[281] Then in the presence of those attending the meeting, Joseph Smith received a revelation now found in Doctrine and Covenants 65.

The Prophet introduced this revelation saying, "In the forepart of October, I received the following Revelation on prayer."[282] Alluding to Daniel's prophecy, this revelation indicated that because "the keys of the kingdom of God are committed unto man on the earth, and from thence shall the gospel roll forth unto the ends of the earth. . . . that his kingdom may go forth upon the earth, that the inhabitants thereof may receive it, and be prepared for the days to come, in the which the Son of Man shall come down in heaven" (verses 2, 5). Regarding this prophecy, the Prophet later stated: "I calculate to be one of the instruments of setting up the Kingdom of Daniel by the word of the Lord, and I intend to lay a foundation that will revolutionize the whole world."[283]

---

280 William E. McLellin, *The Ensign of Liberty of the Church of Christ* 1, no. 4 (January 1848): 61.
281 Shipps and Welch, *Journals of William E. McLellin*, 45.
282 Joseph Smith History, vol. A-1, 155, JSP.
283 Joseph Smith History, vol. F-1, 18, JSP.

The Book of Commandments and
the November 1831 Conference

*Parlor in the Johnson home. A conference was held here in 1831 where the decision was made to publish
Joseph Smith's revelations, making the Johnson home the birthplace of the Doctrine and Covenants.
Photo by Casey Paul Griffiths.*

From the time of the formal organization of the Church in 1830 until
November 1831, obtaining a copy of the Prophet's revelations required traveling to Joseph Smith's home and copying them by hand or by copying someone
else's copy. Orson Pratt recalled, "We often had access to the manuscripts [of
the revelations] when boarding with the Prophet; and it was our delight to read
them over and over again, before they were printed. And so highly were they
esteemed by us, that we committed some to memory; and a few we copied for
the purpose of reference in our absence on missions; and also to read them to
the saints for their edification."[284] However, copying by hand was time-consuming and resulted in numerous errors—everything from simple omissions
or word changes to the adding of new content.

Shortly before November 1831, Joseph and other Church leaders had likely made the decision to publish these revelations into a volume and selected its

---

284   Orson Pratt, "Explanation of Names in the Covenants," *The Seer* 2 (March 1854):
      228.

name—The Book of Commandments. The timing of the decision may have been affected by difficulties following publication in a local newspaper of nine letters written by Ezra Booth criticizing Joseph and the Church. Beginning with the first day of November, Joseph convened a conference concerning the publication of the revelations. This conference would stretch over the following twelve days and be a conduit to receive further revelations, including what would later be found in Doctrine Covenants 1, 67–69, 70, the latter portions of 107, and 133, as well as the testimonies of the witnesses to the Book of the Lord's Commandments.

On the morning of November 1, 1831, the conference began with Oliver Cowdery requesting that the conference determine "the mind of the Lord" as to how many copies to print.[285] The conference boldly decided to publish 10,000 copies—twice the number of the first edition of the Book of Mormon—which suggests they recognized the role the book would play in the Restoration. By comparison, the 1830 publication of the Book of Mormon was considered a very large print to run for any press, especially for one of its size located in a rural community.

Either before or following the decision regarding the number of copies to be printed, the revelation given for Orson Hyde, Luke Johnson, Lyman Johnson, and William E. McLellin, now found in Doctrine and Covenants 68, was probably revealed.[286] In the revelation, the Lord also directed that "other bishops be set apart unto the church, to minister even according to the first [bishop]" (Doctrine and Covenants 68:14). A month later in Kirtland where the Prophet and other brethren were meeting with leading brethren, the Lord revealed that it was "expedient . . . for a bishop to be appointed . . . in this part of the Lord's vineyard," and "Newel K. Whitney is the man who shall be appointed" (Doctrine and Covenants 72:2, 8).

During that morning of November 1, Oliver Cowdery, William E. McLellin, and Sidney Rigdon were assigned to write a preface for the Book of Commandments. When the three brethren presented their effort to the group, it was "picked . . . all to pieces," and conference participants "requested Joseph to enquire of the Lord about it".[287] During or immediately after a midday adjournment, the Prophet led the conference in prayer, after which he "dictated

---

285   Robin Scott Jensen, "From Manuscript to Printed Page: An Analysis of the History of the Book of Commandments and Revelations," *BYU Studies* 48, no. 3 (2009): 18–52, https://byustudies.byu.edu/article/from-manuscript-to-printed-page-an-analysis-of-the-history-of-the-book-of-commandments-and-revelations/.

286   "Historical Introduction," Book of Commandments, 1833, JSP.

287   W. H. Kelley, "Letter from Elder W. H. Kelley," *The Saints Herald* 29, 1882, 67.

by the Spirit the preface. . . . Joseph would deliver a few sentences and Sydney [Rigdon] would write them down, then read them aloud, and if correct, then Joseph would proceed and deliver more."[288] The Lord provided his own preface to his book and called it "my preface unto the book of my commandments" (Doctrine and Covenants 1:6). This revelation was placed at the front of the Book of Commandments, and later, in the first edition Doctrine and Covenants (1835), it retained its primacy as section 1.

Joseph then testified of the great blessing publishing the Lord's revelations would be and asked the brethren whether they were willing to bear testimony of the truthfulness of this book to all the world, much like the three and eight witnesses of the Book of Mormon. "A number of the brethren arose and said that they were willing to testify to the world that they knew that they [the revelations] were of the Lord."[289] A written testimony was revealed, and the following day's sessions began with Oliver Cowdery reading it to the brethren.

It was probably at that point that some of the brethren expressed concerns about the language of the revelations and were hesitant to affix their names to the testimony. The Lord then gave the revelation that later became section 67 of the Doctrine and Covenants. In it, the Lord challenged the "wisest" among the brethren to see whether one or more of them could write any of the revelations with language superior to the Prophet's. William E. McLellin accepted the challenge, inevitably failed, and the reluctant brethren humbled themselves and expressed a willingness to testify.[290]

Two days after receiving the preface to the Book of Commandments, the Lord revealed a concluding section, an appendix, that is now known as section 133. Joseph Smith wrote:

> It had been decided by the conference that Elder Oliver Cowdery should carry the commandments and revelations to Independence, Missouri, for printing, and that I should arrange and get them in readiness by the time that he left, which was to be by the 15th of the month [November] and possibly before. At this time there were many things which the elders desired to know relative to preaching the Gospel to the inhabitants of the earth, and concerning the gathering: and in order to walk by the true light, and be instructed from on high. On the 3rd of November, 1831, I inquired of the Lord and received the following

---

288   Kelley, "Letter from Elder W. H. Kelley."
289   Minutes, November 1–2, 1831, JSP.
290   Joseph Smith History, vol. A-1, 162, JSP.

revelation, which from its importance, and for distinction has since been added to the Book of Doctrine and Covenants, and called the Appendix.[291]

The recording of this revelation in The Book of Commandments does not refer to it as an "appendix," but it may have been understood by the brethren in the conference that it was to serve as such. For example, when Sidney Rigdon made a copy of it, he added the label "an appendix to Revelation." [292] When William W. Phelps first published it in the May 1833 issue of *The Evening and the Morning Star*, he explained that it was known as "the close" or "the Appendix."[293] Unfortunately, the revelation was never published in the Book of Commandments as a result of the 1833 mob violence in Missouri, but Joseph later referred to it as the "appendix" in the 1835 edition of the Doctrine and Covenants because of "its importance, and for distinction."[294]

At the time the first edition of the Doctrine and Covenants was presented to the Church membership in an August 1835 conference for a vote of approval, this appendix appeared as the last section, which was section 100. It was re-numbered as section 133 in the 1876 edition.

On November 11, 1831, the day began with Joseph receiving the revelation later designated as section 69, which directed John Whitmer to accompany Oliver Cowdery in transporting the manuscript of the revelations to Missouri, along with another revelation relating to Church government, later comprising about one-half of section 107. On November 12, Joseph and some of these other brethren were commanded to form a literary firm (Doctrine and Covenants 70) and were charged with overseeing the printing of the Book of Commandments and numerous other printing projects—two newspapers, an almanac, and a hymnal—although printing the latter two was not accomplished until much later.

The series of four conferences focused on publishing the Book of Commandments concluded on November 12, 1831, and the Prophet and Sidney Rigdon resumed their inspired translation of the Bible. Just two and a half weeks later, the Lord directed them to temporarily stop translating in order to deal with the anti-Latter-day Saint sentiment being instigated by former Church members in the Hiram area (see Doctrine and Covenants 71,

---

291   Joseph Smith History, vol. A-1, 166, JSP.
292   "Historical Introduction," Revelation, November 3, 1831 [D&C 133], JSP.
293   William W. Phelps, "Revelations," *The Evening and Morning Star*, May 1833, [1], JSP.
294   Joseph Smith History, vol. A-1, 166, JSP.

section heading). They joined with other missionaries who were already serving in the area, and they aggressively declared and defended the message of the Restoration by "call[ing] upon [their enemies] to meet [them] both in public and in private" (Doctrine and Covenants 71:7).

By January 10, 1832, "much was accomplished in diminishing the unfavorable feelings that had arisen against the Church" (Doctrine and Covenants 73, section heading), and Joseph reported that their work "did much towards allaying the excited feelings which were growing out of the scandalous letters then being published."[295] As a result, Joseph and Sidney were told that it was "expedient to translate again" (Doctrine and Covenants 73:3)

Although the work in response to the revelation now found in section 71 had a positive effect, the stage was set for the animosity and unrest that would culminate in the violence against and tarring of Joseph and Sidney.

"The Vision": Doctrine and Covenants 76

Detail from the upstairs "translation room" where Joseph Smith and Sidney Rigdon saw the vision of the Father and the Son and the different glories of the eternal world. Photo by Acacia E. Griffiths.

On February 12, 1832, Joseph and Sidney received a revelation that would be known as "the Vision" and is now found in Doctrine and Covenants 76.

---

295   Joseph Smith History, vol. A-1, 179, JSP.

Three weeks before the Vision was revealed, Joseph was sustained as president of the high priesthood at a conference in Amherst, Ohio, during which he received two revelations that are now recorded in section 75. He referenced these experiences in his introduction to the Vision as he described the doctrinal conversation he and Sidney had regarding heaven and hell. This conversation led to the conclusion "that many important points touching the salvation of man had been taken from the Bible, or lost before it was compiled," including the notion that "if God rewarded every one according to the deeds done in the body the term 'Heaven,' as intended for the Saints' eternal home, must include more kingdoms than one" (Doctrine and Covenants 76, section heading). Sidney's Reformed Baptist associate, Alexander Campbell, had taught the concept of three kingdoms as early as 1828, along with the specific requirements associated for entrance into each one.[296] Sidney was highly influenced by Alexander, and his teachings in this regard may have played an additional role in Joseph and Sidney's premise that heaven "must include more kingdoms than one."[297]

A few of the introductory verses of section 76 continue the narrative. As implied by the section heading, the conversations between Joseph and Sidney, and possibly other brethren, that preceded the Vision occurred while they were doing the inspired translation of John 5, which taught of only two conditions that follow the judgment—the resurrection of life and of damnation. They were then surprised that the inspiration dictating the translation seemed to leave the basic heaven or hell perspective intact, leading to further conversation during which "the Lord touched the eyes of [their] understandings and they were opened, and the glory of the Lord shone round about" (verse 19).

---

296 Alexander Campbell, *The Christian Baptist*, June 1, 1829, 557–59.

297 Emanuel Swedenborg, a noted eighteenth-century Swedish mystic, nobleman, and scientist, may have also directly or indirectly influenced Joseph and Sidney's conversation (see Emanuel Swedenborg, *Heaven and Hell*, 1758, trans. John C. Alger, 1900, #29, https://sacred-texts.com/swd/hh/hh01.htm; see also J. B. Haws, "Joseph Smith, Emanuel Swedenborg, and Section 76: Importance of the Bible in Latter-day Revelation," in *The Doctrine and Covenants: Revelations in Context*, ed. Andrew H. Hedges, J. Spencer Fluhman, and Alonzo L. Gaskill, 142–67, https://rsc.byu.edu/book/doctrine-covenants-revelations-context).

The Visionary Experience

The translation room in the Johnson home where Joseph Smith and Sidney Rigdon saw the vision now canonized as Doctrine and Covenants 76. Photo by Casey Paul Griffiths.

What is known about the role of the men in the room during the Vision is due in large measure to the meticulous journal writing of Philo Dibble, whose reminisces appear in two accounts. In one he described what approximately twelve other men, including himself, did and did not see: "During the time that Joseph and Sidney were in the spirit and saw the heavens open . . . not a sound nor motion made by anyone but Joseph and Sidney, and it seemed to me that they never moved a joint or limb during the time I was there. . . . I saw the glory and felt the power, but did not see the vision."[298] In another account, Philo recorded their appearance: "Joseph wore black clothes, but at this time seemed to be dressed in an element of glorious white, and his face shone as if it were transparent, but I did not see the same glory attending Sidney."[299]

---

298   Philo Dibble, "Recollections of the Prophet Joseph Smith," *Juvenile Instructor* 27, no.10 (May 1892): 303–4.

299   Philo Dibble, "Philo Dibble's Narrative," in *Early Scenes in Church History*, Faith-Promoting Series 8 (Salt Lake City: Juvenile Instructor Office, 1882; Salt Lake City: Bookcraft, 1968), 81.

Joseph's transfiguration was not an occurrence limited exclusively to this vision. Numerous accounts document that, like others,[300] a change in the Prophet's appearance frequently accompanied his reception of revelation.

Philo indicated the time he spent witnessing Joseph and Sidney was a little over an hour and constituted two-thirds of the total,[301] while Sidney recalled: "We sat for hours in the Visions of heaven around the throne of God & gazed upon the scenes of Eternity."[302]

Joseph and Sidney continued their pre-vision conversation as the Vision itself was unfolded, again described by Philo: "Joseph would, at intervals, say: 'What do I see' as one might say while looking out the window and beholding what all in the room could not see. Then he would relate what he had seen or what he was looking at. Then Sidney replied, 'I see the same.' Presently Sidney would say 'what do I see?' and would repeat what he had seen or was seeing, and Joseph would reply, 'I see the same.'"[303]

Remarkably, they also testified there was a third participant in the conversation that occurred between Joseph and Sidney while the vision was being revealed: "Jesus Christ, who is the Son, whom we saw and with whom we conversed in the heavenly vision" (Doctrine and Covenants 76:14).

Philo also contrasted Joseph and Sidney's appearance during the Vision: "Joseph appeared as strong as a lion, but Sidney seemed as weak as water, and Joseph, noticing his condition smiled and said, 'Brother Sidney is not as used to it as I am.'"[304] Elsewhere, Philo added, "Joseph sat firmly and calmly all the time in the midst of a magnificent glory, but Sidney sat limp and pale, apparently as limber as a rag."[305]

Of all the events that transpired at the Johnson home, one of the most sacred and important was the declaration of Joseph and Sidney when they stated: "And now, after the many testimonies which have been given of him, this is the testimony, last of all, which we give of him: That he lives! For we saw him, even on the right hand of God; and we heard the voice bearing record that he is the Only Begotten of the Father—that by him, and through him, and of him, the worlds are and were created, and the inhabitants thereof are

---

300   Others, including the Savior (Matthew 17:2), Moses (Exodus 34:29; Moses 1:11), Enoch (Moses 7:3); Abinadi (Mosiah 13:5), Nephi and Lehi (Helaman 5:36), and the Nephite disciples (3 Nephi 19:35), all experienced transfiguration in a like manner.

301   Dibble, "Recollections of the Prophet Joseph Smith."

302   Joseph Smith, Journal, April 6, 1844, 63n120, JSP.

303   Dibble, "Recollections of the Prophet Joseph Smith."

304   Dibble, "Philo Dibble's Narrative."

305   Dibble, "Recollections of the Prophet Joseph Smith."

begotten sons and daughters unto God" (Doctrine and Covenants 76:22–24). In the Johnson home in the upstairs revelation room, Joseph and Sidney both saw and conversed with God and declared their testimony and witness to its truthfulness.

Mini-Devotional – "We saw him, even on the right hand of God"

The vision given to Joseph Smith and Sidney Rigdon in the Johnson Home still has a profound impact on millions of people around the world. Joseph and Sidney gazed upon eternity and saw the fate of the righteous, the Sons of Perdition, and everyone in between. What they saw broadened their understanding of the plan of salvation and the mercy of God. Take a few moments to discuss or reflect on the following questions:

How has a knowledge of the plan of salvation impacted your view of this life?

How does it change your view of God to know that there are degrees of salvation instead of just heaven and hell?

Another important part of the vision was the testimony of Joseph and Sidney of the Father and the Son. They wrote, "And now, after the many testimonies which have been given of him, this is the testimony, last of all, which we give of him: That he lives!" (Doctrine and Covenants 76:22). Take a moment to write or reflect on your testimony of Jesus Christ.

- How can you find a similar witness of the divine nature of Jesus Christ?
- How has the knowledge that Jesus lives impacted your life?

Mob Attack at the Johnson Farm

The front porch of the Johnson Home. Joseph Smith preached from these steps the morning after he was tarred and feather by the mob. Photo by Casey Paul Griffiths.

A little over a month after receiving the glorious vision of God and his kingdoms, Joseph Smith experienced one of the greatest trials of his life. On March 24, 1832, a mob of men numbering about thirty gathered at Benjamin Hinckley's brickyard about a mile east of the Johnson home. After laying specific plans, the mobbers blackened their faces, drank some "liquid courage," and split into two groups. One group went to the residence of the Prophet and his family in the Johnson home while the other group went to the residence of Sidney Rigdon and his family.

Sidney and his family were asleep on the second floor of the cabin when the mob broke through the door. They climbed the stairs and dragged Sidney out of bed and down the stairs. The trauma associated with his head bouncing on the frozen ground and possibly the staircase, along with the beating he received, knocked him unconscious and severely injured his head and body. He was beaten and covered with tar.

The other portion of the mob attacked Joseph in the Johnson home. Joseph and Emma, who was about seven weeks pregnant, were up part of the night tending to their adopted ten-month-old twins, Julia and Joseph, who were sick with the measles. Shortly after they fell asleep, the door to the outside burst open and in rushed approximately twelve members of the mob. Amidst Emma's screams, several of them grabbed Joseph by the legs, arms, and hair. He struggled so strenuously that the one holding his hair, Carnot Mason, yanked out a large swath leaving a bald spot. While being carried out the door, Joseph managed to free one leg and kicked Warren Waste and "sent him sprawling in the street."[306] Warren is quoted as saying, "Do not let him touch the ground, or he will run over the whole of us."[307] Joseph recounted: "I was immediately confined again; and they swore by God, they would kill me if I did not be still, which quieted me. As they passed around the house with me, the fellow that I kicked came to me and thrust his hand into my face, (for I hit him on the nose,) and with an exulting horse laugh, muttered, '___ ____ ye; I'll fix ye.' They then seized me by the throat, and held on till I lost my breath."[308]

Joseph fell unconscious and then awakened shortly thereafter while being carried past the body of Sidney Rigdon. Assuming he was dead, Joseph pleaded for his life, "You will have mercy and spare my life, I hope."[309] His plea was met with cursing and derision.

When they arrived at the designated place of seclusion, Joseph's clothes were ripped off of him and one mobber scratched him all over his body remarking, "That's the way the Holy Ghost falls on folks."[310] He was severely kicked and beaten, and then a bucket of tar, which was probably unheated pine sap, was spread over his body. An attempt was made to also jam the wooden paddle used to spread the tar into his mouth, but Joseph writhed away to prevent it from entering his mouth. A doctor among the mob, Richard Dennison, brought along glass vials of "aqua fortis," currently known as nitric acid. Joseph clenched his teeth to prevent the doctor from being able to pour the contents of the vial into his mouth, so the doctor pounded on Joseph's teeth with the vial in an effort to force his mouth open. Instead, he chipped one of Joseph's teeth and the vial broke splashing the burning concoction on Joseph's cheeks. About that time, approaching noises were heard and the mobbers scattered.

306   Johnson, "History of Luke Johnson," 834.
307   George A. Smith, "Historical Discourse," *Journal of Discourses* 11, November 15, 1864, https://journalofdiscourses.com/11/1.
308   Joseph Smith History, vol. A-1, 205–6, JSP.
309   Joseph Smith History, vol. A-1, 205, JSP.
310   Joseph Smith History, vol. A-1, 205, JSP.

The headstone of Symonds Ryder, a disaffected convert who led the mob attack on Joseph Smith and Sidney Rigdon. The grave is located not far from the Johnson Farm. Photo by Casey Paul Griffiths.

When Joseph gained enough strength to walk, he had to pull tar away from his mouth in order to breathe. Then, guided by a small, distant light emanating from the Johnson home, he walked home. "When I came to the door I was naked, and the tar made me look as if I were covered with blood, and when my wife saw me she thought I was all crushed to pieces, and fainted."[311] Members that had gathered at the Johnson home covered him with a blanket and brought him into the house. They had to scrape his skin in order to remove the tar, and they tended to his other wounds, which probably included broken ribs.[312] The next morning was Sunday, and Joseph reported: "With my flesh all scarfied and defaced, I preached to the congregation as usual."[313] Three listeners chose to be baptized and Joseph performed the ordinances that day.

Adding to the grief and heartache of the beating and tarring was the fact that on the night of the attack, young Joseph Murdock Smith, who was suffering from the effects of measles, "received a severe cold, and continued to grow worse" until tragically six days later he died on Friday, March 30."[314]

---

311   Joseph Smith, *History of the Church of Jesus Christ of Latter-day Saints*, ed. B. H. Roberts (Salt Lake City: Deseret News, 1902), 1:263.

312   Writing to his brother William Smith following an altercation between the two of them, Joseph alluded to an injury in his side that William had exacerbated that he had received during the tarring: "Having once fallen in to the hands of a mob, and now been wounded in my side, and now into the hands of a brother, my side gave way" (Joseph Smith to William Smith, circa December 18, 1835, JSP.

313   Joseph Smith History, vol. A-1, 208, JSP.

314   Joseph Smith History, vol. A-1, 209, JSP.

Mini-Devotional – Sharing our Testimony in the Midst of Persecution

The attack at the Johnson home was one of the worst incidents of persecution that Joseph Smith and Sidney Rigdon endured during their entire lives. The mob attack directly contributed to the death of Joseph and Emma's adopted son. Nonetheless, the next day Joseph felt the need to share his witness of Jesus Christ. Because of his willingness to bear testimony, several people were converted and baptized. Take a moment to discuss or reflect on the following questions:

• When have you endured persecution because of your testimony of the gospel?

• Why is it important to still share your testimony in spite of the opposition you might face?

Spring and Summer 1832

On April 1, 1832, a week after Joseph Smith and Sidney Rigdon had been tarred, they joined Newel K. Whitney, Jesse Gause, and Peter Whitmer Jr. in traveling to Missouri. Emma and little Julia Smith moved to Kirtland to live with Elizabeth Ann Whitney, but because of challenges with Ann's aunt, Emma was forced to move from home to home until Joseph returned and found her "very disconsolate."[315]

After his return from Missouri and spending a few days in Kirtland, Joseph, Emma, and Julia returned to the Johnson home around July 1. After Joseph arranged his "affairs," he "recommenced the translation of the scriptures and thus [he] spent most of the summer."[316]

One of the more recent treasures discovered amidst the records of the Church is Joseph's 1832 history written in his own and Frederick G. Williams's handwriting. Although somewhat rough and unpolished, it sheds light on the Prophet's other recorded histories relating to his early prophetic experiences. It represents the first extant recording of some of the early events in the Restoration and was most likely written between July 20 and September 22, 1832, probably in the Johnson home.

---

315   Joseph Smith History, vol. A-1, 209, JSP.
316   Joseph Smith History, vol. A-1, 216, JSP.

The Johnsons' home was no longer a tranquil place to continue writing and translating. The mobs "continued to molest and menace Father Johnson's house for a long time."[317] Many of the Saints living in the Hiram area had moved to Kirtland or Missouri, and on September 12, 1832, exactly one year from their arrival to Hiram, Joseph, Emma, and Julia moved to Kirtland to live in the Newel K. Whitney Store.

The Johnson Home After 1832

The grave of John Johnson located in the cemetery near to the Kirtland Temple. Photo by Acacia E. Griffiths.

In 1833, the Johnsons sold their home in Hiram to the Stevens family and moved to Kirtland. The sale of their farm was finalized in May 1834, and the Johnson family received $3,000 cash plus the Jude Stevens Farm a mile southwest of the temple in Kirtland. Most of the proceeds were consecrated to the Church at a time when its debts could not be paid. The cash was used to finance the Zion's Camp march as well as the purchase of part of the Peter French Farm, where the temple and printing building were eventually built. John Johnson became steward over much of the French Farm property excepting a few lots designated for the temple and for Oliver Cowdery. He managed

---

317   Joseph Smith History, vol. A-1, 209, JSP.

the inn located on the property, which at that point housed a store and was the temporary location of the Church printing press. He sold a great deal of the property and eventually turned the inn back into a tavern, a motel of sorts, and it became known as the Johnson Inn.

The Johnson Farm in Hiram remained in the Stevens family until the Church purchased it in 1956. The house and farm underwent many changes and purposes. In 1996, President Gordon B. Hinckley directed that the home be restored to its 1831–32 appearance. The restoration took about five years to complete. On October 28, 2001, President Hinckley dedicated the home. He prayed, "'We dedicate and consecrate the John Johnson home as a place sacred unto Thee and unto us, as a place in which Thou didst reveal Thyself with Thy Beloved Son. . . . May this home continue now as a reminder to our people from far and near who may come to visit us, that Thou dost live; that Thou dost speak; that Thy Son lives and dost speak; and that a Prophet has record-ed the things which Thou hast spoken on these premises and held them sacred unto us who live in this favored time.'" President Hinckley declared: "'So long as this Church lasts, so long as it goes across the earth, so long as its history is written and known, the John Johnson home will have a prominent place in that history.'" 318

---

318   "President Hinckley Dedicates John Johnson Home," *Ensign*, January 2002s.

OTHER SITES OF HISTORICAL
SIGNIFICANCE IN OHIO

The old lighthouse at Fairport Harbor, Ohio. Many of the Saints gathering to Kirtland travel through Fairport Harbor. Photo by Casey Paul Griffiths.

Because so many wonderful events relating to Church history occurred during the Kirtland era, there are several places that visitors can consider going to experience firsthand something of the spirit of those events. These locations do not have a visitor's center or missionaries to guide you through them, but each holds a significant place in the story of the Restoration in Ohio and are worth your time to visit.

Lake Erie and Fairport Harbor

Many of the Saints obeying to command to gather to the Ohio (Doctrine and Covenants 37:3) first arrived in a area at Fairport Harbor. Fairport Harbor Village is "a charming harbor town . . . perched on the bluffs above the mouth of the Grand River and overlooks two historic lighthouses and one of the finest public beaches in Ohio. Just 30 miles northeast of Cleveland, Fairport Harbor is an easy day trip for those looking to enjoy a day at the beach."[319] The significance of these sites lies in the role they played in providing a highway of sorts for converts gathering to "the Ohio." Indeed, many of the New York saints who were commanded to gather to Ohio in sections 37-39 utilized Lake Erie and Fairport Harbor. Lucy Mack Smith helped to lead one of the groups of New York saints and circumstances related to trying to using the lake in winter time illustrates Lucy's great faith. Lucy's group had met the Colesville group in Buffalo, New York awaiting the ice on Lake Erie to break up so they could use it as a passageway. Responding to her son, Williams' request for her to investigate the poor behavior of the saints then on board the ship they had booked passage on.

> I went to that part of the boat where the principal portion of our company were. There I found several of the brethren and sisters engaged in a warm debate, others murmuring and grumbling, and a number of young ladies were flirting, giggling, and laughing with gentlemen passengers who were entire strangers to them, whilst hundreds of people on shore and on other boats were witnessing this scene of clamor and vanity among our brethren with great interest. I stepped into their midst, "Brethren and sisters," said I, "we call ourselves Saints and profess to have come out from the world for the purpose of serving God at the expense of all earthly things; and will you, at the very onset, subject the cause of Christ to ridicule by your own unwise and improper conduct? You profess to put your trust in God, then how can you feel to murmur and complain as you do? . . . .
>
> Where is your faith? Where is your confidence in God? Do you not know that all things are in his hands, that he made all things and overrules them? If every Saint here would just lift their desires to him in prayer, that the way might be opened before us, how easy it would be for God to cause the ice to break away, and in a moment's time we could be

319   https://fairportharbor.org/

off on our journey. But how can you expect the Lord to prosper you when you are continually murmuring against him? . . .

Now, brethren and sisters, if you will all of you raise your desires to heaven that the ice may be broken before us, and we be set at liberty to go on our way, as sure as the Lord lives, it shall be done." At that moment a noise was heard like bursting thunder. The captain cried out, "Every man to his post," and the ice parted, leaving barely a pathway for the boat that was so narrow that, as the boat passed through, the buckets were torn with a crash from the waterwheel. This, with the noise of the ice, the confusion of the spectators, the word of command from the captain, and the hoarse answering of the sailors, was truly dreadful. We had barely passed through the avenue, when the ice closed together again, and the Colesville brethren were left in Buffalo, unable to follow us.[320]

Lucy Mack Smith's journey to Fairport Harbor is just one of several important historical events linked to this site. Many missionaries passed through the harbor, including the Quorum of the Twelve apostles, who departed here for their first mission to the Eastern States in 1835, and the first missionaries to the British Isles, who left from Fairport Harbor in 1837.

Joseph Smith was also reunited here with his ninety-three-year old grandmother, Mary Duty Smith, who traveled to Ohio from Massachusetts despite failing health and advanced age. Mary expressed a desire to be baptized by her grandson, and to receive a patriarchal blessing from her son, Joseph Smith Sr. Writing about this happy reunion, the Prophet recalled, "My father, three of his brothers [including Asael Jr.], and their mother, met the first time for many years. It was a happy day, for we had long prayed to see our grandmother and uncles in the Church."[321]

Only eleven days after her arrival in Ohio, Mary passed away. Joseph Smith wrote, "my grandmother fell asleep without sickness, pain or regret. She breathed her last about sunset."[322] Lucy Mack Smith added, "Two days after her sons John and Joseph arrived, she [Mary Duty] was taken sick and . . . she died, firm in the faith of the gospel, although she had never yielded obedience

---

320   Lucy Mack Smith, History, 1844–1845, book 11, p. [12]–book 12, p. [2], JSP.

321   "History, 1838–1856, volume B-1 [1 September 1834–2 November 1838] [addenda]," p. 5 [addenda], JSP.

322   "History, 1838–1856, volume B-1 [1 September 1834–2 November 1838] [addenda]," p. 5 [addenda], JSP.

to any of its ordinances."[323] A funeral was held for Mary, with Sidney Rigdon of the First Presidency providing the sermon. She was buried in the cemetery next to the Kirtland Temple.[324]

View from the Old Lighthouse at Fairport Harbor. Photo by Acacia E. Griffiths.

In 2003 the Ensign Peak Foundation placed a plaque near the Fairport lighthouse to honor the more than 3,000 Saints who gathered to Ohio. Frank Sorosy, the mayor of Fairport, helped unveil the marker. A museum exhibit entitled "Fairport Harbor: Gateway to the Gathering" can be found in the Fairport Harbor Museum during Spring and Summer and at the Lake County Historical Society during the Fall and Winter.[325]

323   David F. Boone, "A Most Remarkable Family: The Ohio Legacy of the Asael and Mary Duty Smith Family," in *Regional Studies in Church History: Ohio and Upper Canada,* ed. Guy L. Dorius, Craig K. Manscill, and Craig J. Ostler, (Provo, UT: Religious Studies Center, 2006), 9.

324   Ibid.

325   https://ensignpeakfoundation.org/fairport-harbor/

Mini-devotional: "Where is Your Faith?"

Lucy Mack Smith was able to rally the Saints for their journey on Lake Erie, by asking two powerful questions: "Where is your faith?" and "Where is your confidence in God?" She believed in miracles, and saw a miracle when the blocking the harbor suddenly opened. When we face seemingly insurmountable obstacles, do we think to trust in God, or do we look to our own strength? Take a moment to discuss or ponder the following questions:

- What can you do to show more faith and confidence in God?
- How has God rewarded your faith when you have shown faith and confidence in Him?

Mayfield Baptism Site

The Mayfield Baptism Site is the likely place where a number of early baptisms occurred in the Kirtland area. Photo by Acacia E. Griffiths.

Mayfield, Ohio was the location of one of the original branches in the Kirtland area and an important location for the four missionaries who came to the area in October and November, 1830. On Sunday, November 7, they held a meeting Parley P. Pratt preached, Oliver Cowdery bore testimony as an eyewitness to the truthfulness of the Book of Mormon, and a local Campbellite preacher, Sidney Rigdon, apparently experienced his own spiritual witness because he publicly announced that he would never preach publicly again. At the end of the meeting thirty people were baptized in the Chagrin River.

To get to the baptism site from Kirtland, travel south on 306 (the main street through Kirtland) for about 9 miles, turn east on the Chardon Rd. (Highway 6) and go another 9 miles, turn south on Highway 174 for about 3 or 4 miles, then east on Rogers Road. Access to parking near the river can be found at Rogers Road Field.

Sirenes Burnett Homesite in Orange, Ohio

This home now stands on the site of the Sirenes Burnett home. A conference held here in 1831 was one of the only times that all of the witnesses of the Book of Mormon shared their testimony in one place.
Photo by Acacia E. Griffiths.

Fifteen miles south of Kirtland is the site of the home of Sirenes Burnett in Orange, Ohio. Orange was the home of John and Julia Murdock, early Kirtland pioneer saints. John was one of the great missionaries in Church history and indeed, his missionary efforts was one of the principal reasons the

Church grew so rapidly after the Lamanite missionaries left Kirtland enroute to western Missouri. Julia died giving birth to twins in April 1831, the twins Joseph and Emma Smith adopted after they lost the twins Emma had given birth to on the Morley Farm.

On April 30, 1831, John suffered a terrible loss when his wife, Julia, died just a few hours after giving birth to twins, a boy and a girl. The same day Emma Smith gave birth to two twins, who both passed away. A widower with three other children to care for, John asked Joseph and Emma to adopt the twins, and they gladly did. Joseph and Emma named the female twin Julia after the twins' mother, and they named the male twin Joseph. The infant Joseph died ten months later as a result of exposure suffered during a mob attack on Joseph Smith at the John Johnson home, but Julia eventually became the first Smith child to live to adulthood.[1]

After John received the revelation in section 99, He left on a mission to the East while his three children traveled to Missouri. John recorded the following regarding this revelation: "I then continued with the church preaching to them and strengthening them and regaining my health till the month of Aug. [1832] when I received the Revelation [D&C 99], at which time I immediately commended to arrange my business and provide for my children and sent them up [to] the Bishop in Zion, which I did by the hand of Bro. Caleb Baldwin in Sept [1832]. I have [sic] him ten Dollars a head for carrying up my three eldest children [Orrice C., John R., and Phebe C.]"[2] It was two years before John was reunited with his children, a moment that only happened when John arrived in Missouri as a member of Zion's Camp.[3]

A conference of the Church was held at the Burnett home October 25-26, 1831. Luke Johnson indicates all twelve witnesses to the Book of Mormon bore testimony, the second high priest ordinations in the history of the Church were performed and were twenty-four high priests consecrated themselves and their means to the Church. This was one of the only occasions where every witness of the Book of Mormon was gathered together and bore testimony of the work. The testimony of the witnesses is recorded in the minutes of the meeting:

> Br Joseph Smith, Jr., said we have assembled together to do the business of the Lord and it is through the great mercy of our God that we are spared to assemble together, many of us have went at the command of the Lord in defiance of everything evil, and obtained blessings unspeakable in consequence of which, our names are sealed in the Lambs' Book of life, for the Lord has spoken it. It is the privilege of every Elder to speak of the things of God &c, And could we all come together with one heart

and one mind in perfect faith the vail might as well be rent to day as next week or any other time and if we will but cleanse ourselves and covenant before God, to serve him, it is our privilege to have an assurance that God will protect us at all times

Br. John Whitmer said that a certain clause in the Church Covenants was too much neglected he feared by the brethren, read accordingly.

Br. Joseph Smith jr. said that the order of the High priesthood is that they have power given them to seal up the Saints unto eternal life. And said it was the privilege of every Elder present to be ordained to the High priesthood . . .

Br. Hyrum Smith said that all he had was the Lord's and he was ready to do his will continually . . .

Br. Peter Whitmer jr. said, ~~ever since~~ my beloved brethren, ever since I have had an acquaintance with the writing of God I have [*blank*] eternity with perfect confidence . . .

Br. Samuel Smith said that ever since he had set out to serve the Lord, not to regard the favor of man but the favor of Heaven.

Br. Martin Harris said that he was anxious that all should be saved &c. also read two verses in the book of Revelations, also covenanted to give all for Christ's sake.

Br. David Whitmer said that he felt to declare to this conference that he had consecrated all that was his to the Lord, and also was desirous to do all for the glory of God . . .

Br. Joseph Smith [Sr.] said that he had nothing to consecrate to the Lord of the things of the Earth, yet he felt to consecrate himself and family. Was thankful that God had given him a place among his saints, felt willing to labor for their good.

Br. Hyrum Smith said that he thought best that the information of the coming forth of the book of Mormon be related by Joseph himself to the Elders present that all might know for themselves.

Br. Joseph Smith jr. said that it was not intended to tell the world all the particulars of the coming forth of the book of Mormon, & also said that it was not expedient for him to relate these things &c . . .

Br Joseph Smith Jr said that he intended to do his duty before the Lord and hoped that the brethren would be patient as they had a considerable distance. also said that the promise of God was that the greatest blessings which God had to bestow should be given to those who contributed to the support of his family while translating the fulness of the scriptures; also said until we have perfect love we are liable to fall and when we have a testimony that our names are sealed in the Lamb's Book of life we have perfect love & then it is impossible for false Christs to deceive us. also said that the Lord held the Church bound to provide for the families of the absent Elders while proclaiming the Gospel: further said that the God had often sealed up the heavens because of <u>covetousness</u> in the Church. Said that the Lord would cut his work short in righteousness and except the church receive the fulness of the Scriptures that they would yet fall. [p. 13]

To travel to the site of the conference from Kirtland, travel south on 306 (the main street through Kirtland) for about 12 miles, turn east on Highway 87 and go another 4 miles until you get to the corner of 87 and Chagrin River Road. The Burnett home used to stand on the southeast corner where another home now stands.

North Union Colony of Shakers and Thompson, Ohio

This gate is the only remaining trace of the Shaker colony visited by Sidney Rigdon, Parley P. Pratt, and Leman Copley. Photo by Acacia E. Griffiths.

The area of Cleveland now known as Shaker Heights was originally known as the North Union Colony of Shakers from 1821 to 1889. The term "Shakers" was given to the United Society of Believers in Christ's Second Appearing, sometimes also referred to as Shaking Quakers, because their worship included very energetic shaking as supposedly moved upon the Spirit. The early missionaries to the Lamanites included spent some time with the Shakers during their three-week stay in Northeastern Ohio. An early Kirtland convert, Leman Copley, had been a Shaker, and was very anxious to take missionaries back to his former religious associates. His desires were fulfilled when he was directed in a revelation recorded as Doctrine and Covenants 49 to accompany "Sidney Rigdon and Parley P. Pratt . . . [to] go and preach my gospel which ye have received, even as ye have received it, unto the Shakers" (verse 1). The Lord described their religious perspectives by saying that "they desire to know the truth in part, but not all, for they are not right before me and must needs repent" (verse 2). The heading to the section outlines where their beliefs were in error. "Some of the beliefs of the Shakers were that Christ's Second Coming had already occurred and that He had appeared in the form of a woman, Ann Lee. They did not consider baptism by water essential. They rejected marriage and believed in a life of total celibacy. Some Shakers also forbade the eating of meat."

Detail of the monument to the Shaker community in Shaker Heights. Photo by Acacia E. Griffiths.

The Lord addressed each of these falsehoods in the revelation with this additional direction: "Wherefore, I send you, my servants Sidney and Parley, to preach the gospel unto them. And my servant Leman shall be ordained unto this work, that he may reason with them, not according to that which he has received of them, but according to that which shall be taught him by you my servants; and by so doing I will bless him, otherwise he shall not prosper" (verses 3-4). The three brethren went to the Shakers, presented their message, and were rejected. This experience bothered Leman to the extent that he reneged on a promise to allow the Colesville saints to live on his property in Thompson, Ohio and he forced them to leave after they had accomplished several land improvements that benefitted him. This is the reason the Lord revealed the Colesville saints should move to Zion in section 54. Leman vacillated in his commitment, eventually joining with two splinter groups after the saints left Kirtland, then eventually cutting off all connection with the Restoration.

Visitors to Shaker Heights can travel to the northeast corner of Shaker Boulevard and Lee Road where a gate and an old well are set on a grassy field. Take I-90 from Kirtland then I-90/I-271 for a total of 16 miles, then take exit 29 to Shaker Blvd. You will head north for a bit then go west to Lee Road.

The Oliver and Rosetta Snow Home

The Oliver and Rosetta Snow home is the childhood residence of Lorenzo and Eliza Snow.
Photo by Casey Paul Griffiths.

Shortly after missionaries began proselyting in the Hiram, Ohio area, Oliver and Rosetta Snow, of Mantua, Ohio joined with the saints. They had been followers of Sidney Rigdon and it was Sidney who introduced them to Joseph Smith. They were eventually joined by other family members including their daughter Eliza R. and their son Lorenzo. Lorenzo and Eliza were faithful throughout their lives, whereas Oliver and Rosetta remained with the saints until the Nauvoo persecutions had a negative effect on Oliver. Their home still stands and the current owners are very friendly and love to talk about the history of their home with visitors who contact them in advance prior to visiting. Rather than publish contact information for them, the senior missionaries at the Johnson Home in Hiram, Ohio have the information you need.

Photo of Lorenzo Snow by C.R. Savage. Courtesy Church History Library.

Lorenzo Snow, the fifth president of the Church, was baptized in June 1836. Reflecting on his decision to be baptized, he later said: "I believed they [the Latter-day Saints] had the true religion, and I joined the Church. So far my conversion was merely a matter of reason . . . I was perfectly satisfied that I had done what was wisdom for me to do under the circumstances."[326] Still Lorenzo longed for a spiritual experience to accompany his intellectual conversion to the gospel, writing, "I had had no manifestation, but I expected one."[327] President Snow then described this experience:

This manifestation did not immediately follow my baptism, as I expected . . . But, although the time was deferred, when I did receive it, its realization was more perfect, tangible and miraculous than even my strongest hopes had led me to anticipate. One day while engaged in my studies, some two or three weeks after I was baptized, I began to reflect upon the fact that I had not obtained a *knowledge* of the truth of the work—that I had not realized the fulfillment of

---

326   "The Grand Destiny of Man," *Deseret Evening News,* July 20, 1901, 22; Frank G. Carpenter, "A Chat with President Snow," quoted in *Deseret Semi-Weekly News,* Jan. 5, 1900, 12.

329 Carpenter, "A Chat with President Snow," 12.

the promise: 'He that doeth my will shall know of the doctrine;' [see John 7:17] and I began to feel very uneasy.'

I laid aside my books, left the house and wandered around through the fields under the oppressive influence of a gloomy, disconsolate spirit, while an indescribable cloud of darkness seemed to envelop me. I had been accustomed, at the close of the day, to retire for secret prayer to a grove, a short distance from my lodgings, but at this time I felt no inclination to do so.

The spirit of prayer had departed, and the heavens seemed like brass over my head. At length, realizing that the usual time had come for secret prayer, I concluded I would not forego my evening service, and, as a matter of formality, knelt as I was in the habit of doing, and in my accustomed retired place, but not feeling as I was wont to feel.

I had no sooner opened my lips in an effort to pray, than I heard a sound, just above my head, like the rustling of silken robes, and immediately the Spirit of God descended upon me, completely enveloping my whole person, filling me from the crown of my head to the soles of my feet, and O, the joy and happiness I felt! No language can describe the instantaneous transition from a dense cloud of mental and spiritual darkness into a refulgence of light and knowledge, as it was at that time imparted to my understanding. I then received a perfect knowledge that God lives, that Jesus Christ is the Son of God, and of the restoration of the Holy Priesthood, and the fulness of the gospel.

It was a complete baptism—a tangible immersion in the heavenly principle or element, the Holy Ghost; and even more real and physical in its effects upon every part of my system than the immersion by water; dispelling forever, so long as reason and memory last, all possibility of doubt or fear in relation to the fact handed down to us historically, that the 'Babe of Bethlehem' is truly the Son of God; also the fact that He is now being revealed to the children of men, and communicating knowledge, the same as in the apostolic times. I was perfectly satisfied, as well I might be, for my expectations were more than realized, I think I may safely say, in an infinite degree.

I cannot tell how long I remained in the full flow of this blissful enjoyment and divine enlightenment, but it was several minutes before the celestial element, which filled and surrounded me, began gradually to withdraw. On arising from my kneeling posture, with my heart swelling with gratitude to God beyond the power of expression, I felt—*I knew* that he had conferred on me what only an Omnipotent Being can confer—that which is of greater value than all the wealth and honors worlds can bestow.[328]

Eliza R. Snow enjoyed just as remarkable a career in Church service as her brother. She first met Joseph Smith when he visited the Smith home in the winter of 1831-32. She later remembered that as the Prophet sat by the fire, she "scrutinized his face as closely as I could without attracting his attention and decided that his was an honest face."[329] Eliza attended a meeting where Joseph Smith and two witnesses of the Book of Mormon preached. Soon after, her mother and sister, Rosetta and Leonora, were baptized. But Eliza still waited, continuing to study the Book of Mormon.

Photo of Eliza Roxcy Snow.
Courtesy Church History Library.

It was not until several years later, in the Spring of 1835, that Eliza decided to be baptized. "My heart was now fixed," she later remembered.[330] She was baptized on April 5, 1835 in a stream near to her home. At night after her baptism Eliza reflected: "I felt an indescribable, tangible sensation, ... commencing at my head and enveloping my person and passing off at my feet, producing inexpressible happiness." She then saw a vision of a candle with a long, bright flame, and a voice told her, "The lamp of intelligence shall be lighted over your path."[331]

Eliza later followed the Saints to Missouri, Illinois, and Utah. She served as the first secretary of the Nauvoo Relief Society. She was instrumental in the reorganization of the Relief Society in 1867, serving as its second president. Known as "Zion's poetess" she eventually wrote over 500 poems, including

---

328 *Juvenile Instructor,* Jan. 15, 1887, 22–23.

329 Eliza R. Snow, "Sketch of My Life," in *The Personal Writings of Eliza R. Snow,* ed. Maureen Ursenbach Beecher, (Logan, UT: Utah State University Press, 2000), 9-10.

330 Snow, "Sketch of My Life," 10; see also Salt Lake City 20th Ward, Ensign Stake, Relief Society Minutes and Records, vol. 1, Jul. 10, 1868, 28, Church History Library, Salt Lake City.

331 Snow, "Sketch of My Life," 10.

some of the most beloved hymns of the restoration such as "Oh My Father," "The Time is Far Spent," and "Through Deepening Trials."[332]

Mini-devotional: "The Heavens Seemed Like Brass"

Both gifted writers, Lorenzo and Eliza R. Snow left behind detailed accounts of their conversions to the gospel. Both became important Church leaders, with Lorenzo becoming President of the Church and Eliza serving as the second General Relief Society President. But both explained that their testimony of the gospel did not come in an instant, but took time and effort. Lorenzo even wrote that when he first prayed "the heavens seemed like brass." Eliza also took years until she felt she was ready to be baptized.

Take a moment to reflect on how you gained your testimony of the Gospel. How did it come to you? Did it take time or did it come at once? Take a moment to ponder or write about the following questions:

- Why do you think the Lord sometimes waits to answer our prayers?
- What is the story of your conversion to the Gospel of Jesus Christ?

Amherst, Ohio

Parley P. Pratt lived with his wife, Thankful, in Amherst, Ohio. They left from here when Parley, an associate of the Campbellite preacher, Sidney Rigdon, felt impressed to travel east to preach then felt impressed to get off the canal boat near Palmyra, New York. These inspired decisions resulted in his conversion and shortly thereafter, to his call as one of the four Lamanite missionaries. When he returned to Amherst in that capacity, he was arrested by Elias Peabody, a local law enforcement officer, but managed to escape when he challenged Elias' dog, Stu-boy, to a race. Parley described his escape in his autobiography:

> After sitting awhile by the fire in charge of the officer [Peabody], I requested to step out. I walked out into the public square accompanied by him. Said I, "Mr. Peabody, are you good at a race?" "No," said he, "but

---

332 See Jennifer Reeder, "'My Heart Is Fix'd': Eliza R. Snow's Lifelong Conversion," https://www.churchofjesuschrist.org/study/liahona/2021/02/digital-only/my-heart-is-fixd-eliza-r-snows-lifelong-conversion?lang=eng#note6

my big bulldog is, and he has been trained to assist my office these several years; he will take any man down at my bidding." "Well, Mr. Peabody, you compelled me to go a mile, I have gone with you two miles. You have given me an opportunity to preach, sing, and have also entertained me with lodging and breakfast. I must now go on my journey; if you are good at a race you can accompany me. I thank you for all your kindness — good day, sir."

I then started on my journey, while he stood amazed and not able to step one foot before the other. Seeing this, I halted, turned to him and again invited him to a race. He still stood amazed. I then renewed my exertions, and soon increased my speed to something like that of a deer. He did not awake from his astonishment sufficiently to start in pursuit till I had gained, perhaps, two hundred yards. I had already leaped a fence, and was making my way through a field to the forest on the right of the road. He now came hallooing after me and shouting to his dog to seize me. The dog, being one of the largest I ever saw, came close on my footsteps with all his fury; the officer behind still in pursuit, clapping his hands and hallooing, "Stu-boy, Stu-boy — take him — watch — lay hold of him, I say — down with him," and pointing his finger in the direction I was running. The dog was fast overtaking me, and in the act of leaping upon me, when, quick as lightning, the thought struck me, to assist the officer, in sending the dog with all fury to the forest a little distance before me. I pointed my finger in that direction, clapped my hands, and shouted in imitation of the officer. The dog hastened past me with redoubled speed towards the forest, being urged by the officer and myself, and both of us running in the same direction.

Gaining the forest, I soon lost sight of the officer, and dog, and have not seen them since. I took a back course, crossed the road, took round into the wilderness, on the left, and made the road again in time to cross a bridge over Vermillion River, where I was hailed by half a dozen men, who had been anxiously waiting our arrival to that part of the country, and who urged me very earnestly to stop and preach. I told them that I could not then do it, for an officer was on my track. I passed on six miles farther, through mud and rain, and overtook the brethren, and preached the same evening to a crowded audience, among whom we were well entertained.[333]

---

333   Parley P. Pratt, *Autobiography of Parley P. Pratt,* (Salt Lake: Deseret Book, 1985), 36-39.

In November 1831, the Lord directed that "it must needs be that one be appointed of the High Priesthood to preside over the priesthood, and he shall be called President of the High Priesthood of the Church; Or, in other words, the Presiding High Priest over the High Priesthood of the Church. . . . And again, the duty of the President of the office of the High Priesthood is to preside over the whole church, and to be like unto Moses—Behold, here is wisdom; yea, to be a seer, a revelator, a translator, and a prophet, having all the gifts of God which he bestows upon the head of the church" (Doctrine and Covenants 107:65-66, 91-92). On January 25 following, Joseph convened a conference in Amherst "at which [he] was sustained and ordained President of the High Priesthood" (Doctrine and Covenants 75:heading) and where he received two revelations now combined into section 75. Joseph was later similarly sustained at a conference in Missouri (see section 82), and these two events represent important inspired steps toward the eventual establishment of the First Presidency (see also sections 81 and 90).

Parley and Thankful lived in two homes near the corner of Russia Road and Rt. 58 in present day Amherst. Take I-90 west from Kirtland for about 60 miles then take the Highway 58 exit and go south for about 3 miles to Russia Road. The Amherst town square is the modern-day location of Parley's Stu-boy race.

Timeline of the Kirtland Apostasy:

- On November 2, 1836 Church leaders drew up article for the Kirtland Safety Society.

- On January 2, 1837 the Kirtland Safety Society opened for business.

- By November 1837 the Kirtland Safety Society ceased operations.

- Fall 1837 marked a period of severe apostasy for the Church.

- On January 12, 1838 Joseph Smith and Sidney Rigdon fled from Kirtland, fearing for their lives.

- On July 6, 1838 the Kirtland Camp, a collection of faithful Saints left Kirtland.

- On January 19, 1841 Joseph Smith received a revelation where the Lord proclaimed a "scourge prepared" for the inhabitants of Kirtland (see Doctrine and Covenants 124:83).

- On October 14, 1979 Apostle Ezra Taft Benson proclaimed that the scourge on Kirtland was lifted.

- On April 3, 2022 President Russell M. Nelson announced the construction of the Cleveland, Ohio temple.

Epilogue

"I, the Lord, Will Build Up Kirtland"

Kirtland Safety Society, Exodus, Scourge, and Return to Kirtland

The Kirtland Temple at sunset.. Photo by Acacia E. Griffiths.

In 1836 the Saints were enjoying life in Kirtland with a newly dedicated temple and a large migration of Saints to the area. Things looked bright and hopeful. However, amongst church leaders there was a growing concern over the economy of Kirtland and the financial stability of the church. Land speculation, due to the ever-increasing migration of saints to the area and the growing economies of other communities in the Western Reserve, drove up the price of property and the cost of purchasing a home and other goods. With the increased number of people looking for employment the average income of workers was decreasing, and more people were extending themselves on credit. Many of the saints who arrived in the area had sold their homes and belongings at a discounted price to migrate to be with the Saints. Most of the value of their assets were in land values and other non-liquid assets that made cash flow a difficult prospect. The church was also experiencing a similar problem with the majority of their debts in the form of 90-to-180-day notes while their assets were primarily in nonliquid lands.[334]

To alleviate the cash flow problem and help stabilize the economy of Kirtland and the financial challenges of the church, Joseph Smith and other church leaders desired to establish a bank in Kirtland. In the fall of 1836 church leaders drew up a charter for a bank, the Kirtland Safety Society.[335] However, the Ohio State legislature driven by hard-money politicians was rejecting almost all bank applications in Ohio in 1836-1837.[336] Soon church leaders recognized the futility of establishing a bank given the political climate and instead revised their Article of Agreement and on January 2, 1837 Church leaders changed the name of the "Kirtland Safety Society" and formed a joint-stock company called the "Kirtland Safety Society Anti-Banking Company," They began issuing "anti-banking" notes in payment of church obligations.[337] Between January and November of 1837 it is estimated about $100,000 in notes was issued by the Kirtland Safety Society.[338] The US Constitution states that only Congress has the power to create money and in the 1830's the Treasury Department issued gold and silver coins known as specie. At this time, it was also common practice for businesses to lend money in the form of banknotes that were printed and used much like promissory notes. These notes were backed by small amounts of specie and large amounts of less liquid forms of capital like land or merchandise.[339] The Ohio State legislature began implementing laws limiting these uncharted banks operations and the legality of these institutions was still in question during the time of the formation of the Kirtland Safety Society.

---

334   Sampson, D. Paul, and Larry T Whitmer, "The Kirtland Safety Society: The Stock Ledger Book and the Bank Failure." *BYU Studies,* 12 (summer 1972) 427-36.

335   Ibid.

336   Ibid.

337   Adams, Dale W. "Chartering the Kirtland Bank." *BYU Studies*, 23 (Fall 1983): 467-82.

338   Ibid.

339   Staker, 447.

Within a few weeks of the first issuance of notes and the opening of its doors, there was opposition to the Kirtland Safety Society by those who sought for its failure to promote their own financial interests and by increasing doubt of its success and viability by many of the Saints. In a meeting in the Kirtland Temple, Joseph stated, "We have plenty of every thing necessary to our comfort and convenience…But brethren beware for I tell you this I[n] the name of the Lord that there is an evil in this very congregation which if [it] is not repented of will result in something very [like] an apostasy making one third of you who are here this day so much my enemies that you will have a desire to take my life and even would do so if God permitted the deed." [340]

Although he earlier prophesied of the Safety Society's prosperity, this suggests that due to the "evil" amongst the saints, he now had uncertainty about its eventual success. Wilford Woodruff recorded that, "many of the church had refused Kirtlan[d] Currency which was their temporal salvation in Consequence of thus they put strength in the hands of their enemies & those that had done this thing must suffer by it."[341] Although Joseph and the other leaders continued to invest their own finances in the society and continued to seek financing to help cover the demand of the run on the specie, within a month of its opening, demand for redemption of specie had depleted the societies small reserve.[342]

Adding to the challenges of the Kirtland Safety Society were the larger economics of the United States and its politics. Recent laws had been passed fueled by a desire for reform on the banking system. These pressures and actions at the federal and local levels lead to the financial Panic of 1837. Many of the banks throughout the nation began closing in March. [343] The nationwide crisis was evident in June when many banks failed and closed. This caused the bank notes of the Kirtland Safety Society to become practically worthless overnight.[344] Joseph Smith and most of his family turned their stocks over to the care Oliver Granger and Jared Carter. The Society continued to operate in order to try and cover its debts and satisfy its creditors but eventually closed its doors in November 1837.[345]

---

340 Anderson, Lucy's Book, 594 as found in Staker, 486.
341 Wilford Woodruff's Journal April 9, 1837, quoted in in Staker, 522.
342 Sampson, D. Paul, and Larry T Whitmer, "The Kirtland Safety Society: The Stock Ledger Book and the Bank Failure." BYU Studies 12 (summer 1972) 427-36.
343 Staker, 497.
344 Ibid., 500.
345 Ibid., 28.

Aftermath of the Kirtland Safety Society

With the difficulties of the Kirtland Safety Society, some Saints began losing their faith in Joseph Smith and the church, while many others were strengthened amidst the opposition. During the spring of 1837 Joseph and Sydney fled Kirtland and went into hiding in Palmyra. NY. Concerning Joseph, Wilford Woodruff recorded that, "his life was so beset & sought for by wicked and ungodly men for the testimony of JESUS, that he was under the necessity of fleeing his house & home for a few days."[346] Many claimed that Joseph had promised that the Kirtland Safety Society had been instituted by the will of God and were promised that it would not fail. Some of his accusers brought charges against him for lying, misrepresentation, and extortion.[347] There are no records to indicate that Joseph stated that the society would never fail. Earlier he had encouraged the saints to invest in the society and if they followed the commandments, they and the institution would be blessed. In January 1837 edition of the Messenger and the Advocate Joseph quoted an earlier revelation from 1833 (D&C 107:72-73) about gathering money for the building up of Zion. He then encouraged "the brethren from abroad, to take stock in the Safety Society."[348]At a meeting on April 6, 1837 Wilford Woodruff recorded that, "Joseph desired…that we must keep in view the institution of the Kirtland Safety Society & if the Elders of Israel would be faithful & do what was in their power this once Kirtland should spedily be redeemed & become a strong hold not to be thrown down" "as it was given him by revelation."[349] For some this lead to a misunderstanding of the Society and caused them to loose faith.

In the Fall of 1837 a group led by Warren Parrish rejected the First Presidency and declared Joseph Smith a fallen prophet. They called themselves "the Church of Christ."[350] Another group met in the Kirtland Temple with "several of the Twelve" to depose the Prophet Joseph and appoint a different President of the Church. Brigham Young was in attendance and recorded:

---

346   Wilford Woodruff's Journal April 13, 1837 quoted in Staker, 522-523.
347   Mark L Staker, *Hearken, O Ye People: The Historical Settings of Joseph Smith's Ohio Revelations*, (Midvale: Greg Kofford Books, 2009), 527.
348   Ibid., 520
349   Wilford Woodruff's Journal April 9, 1837, quoted in Staker, 521.
350   Staker, 535.

I rose up, and in a plain and forceable manner told them that Joseph was a Prophet, and I knew it, an that they might rail and slander him as much as they pleased, they could not destroy the appointment of the Prophet of God, they could only destroy their own authority, cut the thread that bound them to the prophet and to God and sink themselves to hell...This was a crisis when earth and hell seemed leagues to overthrow the Prophet and Church of God. The knees of many of the strongest men in the Church faltered.[351]

The disaffection spread through many church members including the highest councils of the church. On September 3rd, Joseph called for a conference of the church and sought to have a sustaining vote of the First Presidency, Quorum of the Twelve Apostles, and other quorums of the church. At this meeting, three of the Quorum of the Twelve Apostles, Luke Johnson, Lyman Johnson, and John F Boynton were "rejected & cut off" from their position in the quorum.[352] John F Boynton protested and stated that his concern was justified "by reason of the failure of the Bank" and stated "that he had understood the Bank was instituted by the will of God, and he had been told that it never should fail let men do what they would.[353]" After the protest by John F Boynton, Joseph arose and stated, "that if this had been declared, no one had authority from him for so doing, For he had always said unless the institution was conducted on richeous [righteous] principals it would not stand.[354]" At this meeting John Johnson was also removed from his office on the High Council. At a conference on Sept 10th Luke Johnson, Lyman Johnson, and John F Boynton confessed their errors and were reinstated into the church and retained their calling as Apostles.

The troubles and hostilities continued to plague Joseph and the Church. That Fall more lawsuits and cases were brought against church leaders and the voice of opposition and apostasy strengthened amongst a growing number of disaffected church members. In late December the High Council excommunicated 28 members including Martin Harris, Warren Parrish, and apostles Luke Johnson and John F. Boynton.

351   "History of Brigham Young," DNW, 10 Feb. 1858, 386
352   "Journal, March–September 1838," p. 20, JSP.
353   "Journal, March–September 1838," p. 21, JSP.
354   Ibid.

Kirtland Exodus and Scourge

On January 12, 1838, Joseph received three revelations, one directing the First Presidency to leave Kirtland:

> Thus saith the Lord Let the presidency of my Church take their families as soon as it is praticable and a door is open for them and move on to the west as fast as the way is made plain before their faces and let their hearts be comforted for I will be with them
>
> Verily I say unto you the time [has] come that your laibours are finished in this place, for a season, Therefore arise and get yourselves on to a land which I shall show unto you even a land flowing with milk and honey[355]

The revelation stated, "let all your faithful friends arise with their families also and get out of this place and gather themselves together unto Zion.[356]" That evening at 10pm Joseph Smith and Sidney Rigdon left Kirtland to never return. Of this event Joseph stated, "A new year dawned upon the church in Kirtland in all the bitterness of the spirit of apostate Mobocracy; which continued to rage and grow hotter and hotter until Elder [Sidney] Rigdon and myself were obliged to flee from its deadly influence.[357] They traveled all night and arrived at 8am in Medina 60 miles to the south. Their families joined them a few days later and they traveled toward Farr West, Missouri. Many of the saints in Kirtland began preparing to leave and join the Saints in Missouri. About 822 Saints organized under the direction of the presidency of the seventy into the Kirtland Camp and left Kirtland on July 6, 1838.[358]

Two days after the Kirtland Camp departed, Joseph received a revelation directing Newel Whitney and Williams Marks to "settle up their business speedily and journey from the land of Kirtland (D&C 117:1)" In that revelation the saints were also commanded to "let the properties in Kirtland be turned out for debts" and "let them go (vs 5)." They were also told to "come up hither unto the land of my people, even Zion (vs 9)." In this revelation Oliver Granger was also directed to settle the affairs of the First Presidency.

---

355   "Revelation, 12 January 1838–C," p. [1], The Joseph Smith Papers, JSP.
356   Ibid.
357   "History, 1838–1856, volume B-1 [1 September 1834–2 November 1838]," p. 780, JSP.
358   Staker, 551.

The Kirtland Saints were also told to "remember the Lord their God, and mine house also, to keep and preserve it holy, and to overthrow the moneychangers in my own due time (vs 16)."

Most of the saints left Kirtland in the spring and summer of 1838 but the migration continued for years. Some saints remained and continued to gather in congregations throughout the region. On October 3, 1840 at a General Conference of the Church in Nauvoo, Illinois, Joseph stood "and stated that it was necessary that something, should be done with regard to Kirtland, so that it might be built up and gave it as his opinion, that the brethren from the east might gather there, and also, that it was necessary that someone should be appointed from this conference to preside over that stake."[359] Joseph called Almon Babbitt to serve as stake president of Kirtland and help establish it as a gathering place for the saints. Almon quickly began petitioning the English saints to come to Kirtland even though they were already headed to Nauvoo. He also created an iron mill and announced plans to publish a newspaper. His over energetic leadership alarmed Joseph and just three months after being called to preside, on January 19, 1841 Joseph received a revelation concerning Kirtland. "I, the Lord, will build up Kirtland, but I, the Lord, have a scourge prepared for the inhabitants thereof. And with my servant Almon Babbitt, there are many things with which I am not pleased; behold, he aspireth to establish his counsel instead of the counsel which I have ordained, even that of the Presidency of my Church; and he setteth up a golden calf for the worship of my people (D&C 124:83-84)." Later on October 31, 1841 Hyrum received further revelation concerning the scourge of Kirtland: "Thus saith the Lord;" therefore pay out no monies, nor properties for houses, nor lands, in that Country, for if you do, you will lose them; for the time shall come, that you shall not possess them in peace; but shall be scourged with a sore scourge; yet your children may possess them; but not until many years shall pass away."[360]

Although the Lord declared a scourge upon the inhabitants of Kirtland he also gave hope that He would "build up Kirtland" and that the "children" of those who left behind their beloved city would again one day "possess" the land of Kirtland.

359   "Minutes and Discourse, 3–5 October 1840," p. 185, JSP.
360   "History, 1838–1856, volume C-1 [2 November 1838–31 July 1842]," p. 1242, JSP.

The Building Up of Kirtland

The Stake Center in Kirtland. Photo by Casey Paul Griffiths.

The night before the Joseph Smith's death he dreamed of his farm in Kirtland. "I was back in Kirtland, Ohio, and thought I would take a walk out by myself, and view my old farm, which I found grown up with weeds and brambles, and altogether bearing evidence of neglect and want of culture. I went into the barn, which I found without floor or doors, with the weatherboarding off, and was altogether in keeping with the farm. While I viewed the desolation around me and was contemplating how it might be recovered from the curse upon it there came rushing into the barn a company of furious men, who commenced to pick a quarrel with me."[361] The dream continued with Joseph escaping the barn when the group of men began fighting each other. When Joseph was a "distance from the barn" he "heard them screeching

---

361   "History, 1838–1856, volume F-1 [1 May 1844–8 August 1844]," p. 177, JSP.

and screaming" of the men who were engaged in a "fight with their knives."[362] Years after leaving and even while imprisoned, Joseph continued to reflect on Kirtland and wondered when the curse would be lifted.

Although the early saints fled, the Lord continued to "build up Kirtland." On May 2, 1954, President David O McKay dedicated the first church building in Northern Ohio since the exodus of the Saints. President McKay also directed the purchasing of the Historic Johnson Home in Hiram in 1856. On October 14, 1979, President Ezra Taft Benson, president of the Quorum of the Twelve Apostles, presided over the ground breaking of the first meetinghouse in Kirtland.[363] While there he declared, "the scourge that was placed upon the people in that prophecy [D&C 124:83] is being lifted today." "Our prophecy said that yet your children may possess the Kirtland Lands, but not until many years shall pass away. Those many years have, I feel, passed away, and now is the time. Now is the time to arise and shine and look forward to great progress in this part of the Lord's vineyard." [364] In 1984 President Benson dedicated the newly restored Newel K Whitney store. In 2001 President Gordon B Hinckley dedicated the Historic Johnson Home and in 2003 he dedicated all of Historic Kirtland. [365]

In the April 2022 General Conference President Russell M Nelson announced that a temple would be built in Cleveland, Ohio.[366] The Lord's promise to once again "build up Kirtland" is continuing to roll forth.

362   "History, 1838–1856, volume F-1 [1 May 1844–8 August 1844]," p. 177, JSP.

363   Karl Ricks Anderson, Joseph Smith's Kirtland: Eyewitness Accounts 1989 Deseret Book, 246-247.

364   Ezra Taft Benson, address at groundbreaking for the Kirtland Ward meetinghouse, October 17, 1982, ms., LDS Archives. As quoted in Karl Ricks Anderson, Joseph Smith's Kirtland: Eyewitness Accounts 1989 Deseret Book, 247.

365   Karl Ricks Anderson, *Joseph Smith's Kirtland: Eyewitness Accounts*, (Salt Lake City: Deseret Book, 1989), 246-250.

366   Russell M Nelson, "Now is the Time," April 2022 General Conference.

About the Authors

THOMAS AARDEMA is a Region Director of Seminaries and Institutes with his office near the Johnson Home. He has taught seminary and institute for 20 years and has lived and taught in the Kirtland area for 9 years. He received a BA of History from Weber State University, an MBA from the University of Utah, and a PhD in Education from Utah State University. He and his wife Emilee are the parents of 5 sons. He loves church history and feels blessed to live and teach near the sacred sites of Kirtland.

DAMON L. BAHR is an associate professor in the Department of Teacher Education at Brigham Young University where he teaches courses in how to teach mathematics to young children. He also teaches Doctrine and Covenants courses in the Department of Church History and Doctrine at BYU and has been teaching about Kirtland Church history in Campus Education Week for the last six years. This volume is his second book related to the Kirtland era of Church history he and his co-author have written. The first, also published by Cedar Fort, is entitled *The Voice of the Lord is Unto All Men: A Remarkable Year of Revelations in the Johnson Home* and is the first of a series of five involving the revelations give to the Prophet Joseph Smith in and around the places he lived in Kirtland that are in various stages of production. The eternal family he and his beloved wife, Kim, started 46 years ago has grown to 28 at last count, and the two of them were privileged to serve a mission in Kirtland.